Short Studies in Private International Law

Short Studies in Private International Law are short-book publications devoted to topics in private international law, in particular international and European civil procedure. The volumes can be a result of papers presented at conferences but can also consist of short monographs or edited volumes on private international law, aimed to inform academics and practitioners timely of recent developments. The hardcover books are compact volumes of 100–150 pages and are characterized by fast, global electronic dissemination, standard publishing contracts, standardized manuscript preparation and formatting guidelines, and expedited production schedules.

More information about this series at http://www.springer.com/series/15450

Vesna Lazić · Steven Stuij
Editors

Recasting the Insolvency Regulation

Improvements and Missed Opportunities

Editors
Vesna Lazić
Private International Law
T.M.C. Asser Institute
The Hague, The Netherlands

Steven Stuij
Erasmus School of Law
Hardinxveld-Giessendam, The Netherlands

ISSN 2522-8145   ISSN 2522-8153   (electronic)
Short Studies in Private International Law
ISBN 978-94-6265-362-7   ISBN 978-94-6265-363-4   (eBook)
https://doi.org/10.1007/978-94-6265-363-4

Published by T.M.C. ASSER PRESS, The Hague, The Netherlands www.asserpress.nl
Produced and distributed for T.M.C. ASSER PRESS by Springer-Verlag Berlin Heidelberg

This T.M.C. ASSER PRESS imprint is published by the registered company Springer-Verlag GmbH, DE part of Springer Nature.
The registered company address is: Heidelberger Platz 3, 14197 Berlin, Germany

Contents

Chapter 1
Insolvency Forum Shopping, Revisited

Wolf-Georg Ringe

Contents

Abstract Over the past several years, European firms have been active in cross-border regulatory arbitrage to benefit from a more favourable bankruptcy regime. The European Insolvency Regulation (EIR), an instrument determining the competent courts and the applicable law in EU cross-border insolvency proceedings, has long sought to curb such efforts. A major reform which came into force in 2017 has the specific objective of further restricting abusive versions of forum shopping, in particular by introducing a three-month 'suspension period' for forum shopping activities carried out shortly before the debtor files for insolvency. This chapter demonstrates that these efforts fail to achieve a satisfactory response to forum shopping. The reform started from the sensible proposition to distinguish between beneficial and 'abusive' variants of forum shopping. However, the key element of the reform, the suspension period, is both over-inclusive and

This chapter draws heavily on my commentary on EIR Article 3 in Bork and van Zwieten 2016.

W.-G. Ringe (✉)
Institute of Law & Economics, University of Hamburg, Johnsallee 35, 20148 Hamburg, Germany
e-mail: georg.ringe@uni-hamburg.de

© T.M.C. ASSER PRESS and the authors 2020
V. Lazić and S. Stuij (eds.), *Recasting the Insolvency Regulation*, Short Studies in Private International Law,
https://doi.org/10.1007/978-94-6265-363-4_1

1

under-inclusive in its scope of application and may, at best, be entirely without effect. But even then, the new rule will also create significant uncertainty and undermine effective ways of business restructuring. At the same time, the reform does not address new variants of forum shopping, such as the use of the British 'scheme of arrangement' by continental European firms. Such 'procedural' forum shopping may be effected entirely without any physical relocation, as it does not come within the scope of application of the EIR Recast. The laudable goal of the EIR Recast to improve the pricing of risks in cross-border insolvencies is jeopardised where the rules on jurisdiction are unclear or uncertain. The 2017 reform is a missed opportunity to improve the system by attaching substantive bankruptcy law and jurisdiction to a company's registered office as the only clear and predictable connecting factor. Instead, the reform introduces new riddles and inconsistencies. Such steps will blur rather than improve the pricing of insolvency risk and thereby ultimately drive up the cost of capital.

Keywords European Insolvency Regulation · forum shopping · centre of main interests · suspension period · scheme of arrangement

1.1 Introduction

Under the regime of the European Insolvency Regulation (EIR Recast),[1] the location of the debtor's 'Centre of Main Interests' (COMI) is the determining factor for both the competent insolvency court as well as the applicable insolvency law. Under the official definition, the debtor's COMI is the 'place where the debtor conducts the administration of his interests on a regular basis and which is ascertainable by third parties'.[2] This definition itself is not overly helpful, and there has been much controversy over its precise scope. Article 3 EIR Recast therefore seeks to flesh out the details for determining the COMI by providing further guidance in the form of three presumptions, distinguishing between different types of debtors. For companies, the main focus of this chapter, the place of the registered office is presumed to be the company's COMI in the absence of proof to the contrary.[3] This presumption can however be rebutted if ascertainable factors suggest that the

---

[1] Regulation (EU) 2015/848 of the European Parliament and of the Council of 20 May 2015 on insolvency proceedings (recast) [2015] OJ L141/19 ('EIR 2015').
[2] Article 3(1) EIR Recast 2015. This corresponds almost exactly to the wording previously found in recital 13 to the original EIR. There are small linguistic differences. The 2015 version says 'shall' and not 'should', and omits 'therefore'. It does not appear that any consequences are connected to these minor changes. Using the former recital came at the suggestion by European Parliament 2011, para 2.2.
[3] Article 3(1) subpara 2 EIR Recast 2015.

debtor's centre of main interest is located in another Member State.[4] Codifying previous case-law, new recital 30 clarifies and confirms that the presumption can be rebutted 'if the company's central administration is located in another Member State than its registered office and a comprehensive assessment of all the relevant factors establishes, in a manner that is ascertainable by third parties, that the company's actual centre of management and supervision and of the management of its interests is located in that other Member State'.[5]

Crucially for present purposes, the Regulation does not specify the relevant point in time for the determination of the COMI. This has led to numerous attempts by debtors to relocate the COMI to another jurisdiction just before the debtor applies for insolvency protection, with the objective of profiting from another court and another substantive law.[6] For example, during the 2000s, a number of cases made headlines where a debtor company physically shifted its COMI to another country prior to the initiation of insolvency proceedings with the objective of seeking insolvency jurisdiction in a country the legal system of which appeared more favourable for its restructuring plans.[7] In particular, a number of German firms moved their COMI to the United Kingdom in order to profit from English insolvency law that they considered to be more helpful for their purposes than German insolvency law. Academic debate considered whether these strategic moves were legitimate or not.[8]

The EIR Recast has always taken a rather critical stance towards forum shopping. Recital 4 of the original version of the EIR Recast holds that 'It is necessary for the proper functioning of the internal market to avoid (...) forum shopping.'[9] When consulted on the revision of the EIR Recast, almost half of the respondents indicated evidence of abusive relocation of a COMI.[10] The revised EIR, which came into force in 2015, therefore includes a number of elements designed to further contain abusive COMI-shifting.[11]

This chapter assesses the merits of the 2015 reform. As we shall see, the reform started on the helpful conceptual distinction between beneficial and abusive forum

---

[4] Case C-341/04 *Eurofood IFSC Ltd* [2006] ECR I-3813, ECLI:EU:C:2006:281, para 34. See also case C-396/09 *Interedil Srl v Fallimento Interedil Srl, Intesa Gestione Crediti SpA* [2011] ECR I-9915, ECLI:EU:C:2011:671, para 52; case C-444/07 *MG Probud Gdynia sp z o o* [2010] ECR I-417, ECLI:EU:C:2010:24, para 37.

[5] The Commission had deliberately introduced the *Interedil* language in recital 13a of its original proposal. See European Commission 2012a, Sect. 3.1.2.

[6] Another version would be to shift the COMI between application for insolvency and the court's opening decision. See on this Ringe 2016, paras 3.73 ff.

[7] See Ringe 2008.

[8] From the ample literature, consider Ringe 2008; McCormack 2009, 2010; Eidenmüller 2011; Mevorach 2013; de Weijs and Breeman 2014.

[9] Council Regulation (EC) No. 1346/2000 of 29 May 2000 on insolvency proceedings, [2000] OJ L160/1.

[10] European Commission 2012a, p. 4; European Commission 2012b, Sect. 3.4.1.

[11] See recitals 29–34 EIR Recast.

shopping. However, the key element of the reform, the suspension period before the insolvency application, suffers from a number of fundamental flaws. At best, it will not have any effect on cross-border COMI shifts at all. At the same time, the EIR does not apply to more recent developments. For example, using an English scheme of arrangement to restructure a continental firm remains entirely outside of the scope of the EIR altogether; the 2015 reform leaves the UK free to define its own jurisdiction test for this procedure.

This chapter proceeds as follows: Sect. 1.2 sets out to discuss the different types of forum shopping in an insolvency context. Subsequently, Sect. 1.3 analyses the key elements of the 2015 EIR reform, and Sect. 1.4 demonstrates the particular problems involved with the introduction of the new suspension period. Section 1.5 then shows how and why schemes of arrangement remain unaffected by the reform and the EIR generally. Section 1.6 concludes.

1.2 Forum Shopping Strategies

In order to understand the impact of the 2015 reform, we first need to clarify the specific design of forum shopping operations. Two main strategies appear to be mostly used. In some situations, the corporate debtor seeks to move its registered office (plus, sometimes, any additional operations) to another country. This is because of the presumption, found in Article 3 of the EIR, according to which the registered office of a company or legal person normally corresponds to its COMI. Relocation of the registered office would thus change the relevant insolvency jurisdiction under Article 3 and simultaneously change the applicable substantive insolvency law under Article 7 of the revised EIR. A real-world example of that strategy is the transformation by Deutsche Nickel AG (DNick) from being a German public limited company to becoming an English private limited company with a registered office in the UK.[12] Alternative routes for this strategy would be the formal 'seat transfer' mechanism under the Societas Europaea regime[13] or the framework offered under the Cross-Border Merger Directive.[14]

The second strategy would be to simply move the effective 'head office functions' of a company abroad, whilst leaving the registered office behind. For example, the company may remain incorporated where it was, but the management and the board of directors may move to a new Member State. This strategy seeks to convince the courts that the presumption should be rebutted and that the centre of main interests has been moved to the new 'head office' Member State, irrespective

---

[12] See on this Ringe 2008, pp. 586–587.
[13] Council Regulation (EC) No. 2157/2001 of 8 October 2001 on the Statute for a European company, [2001] OJ L294/1, Article 8.
[14] Directive 2005/56/EC of the European Parliament and of the Council of 26 October 2005 on cross-border mergers of limited liability companies, [2005] OJ L310/1.

of the registered office. This approach can be exemplified by *Hellas Telecommunications*, where the English courts held that the COMI of *Hellas Telecommunications (Luxembourg) II SCA* had been effectively transferred from Luxemburg to England despite the fact that the company's registered office remained in Luxembourg.[15]

For individuals, the equivalent to the 'registered office' is the 'principal place of business' or the 'habitual residence'. These criteria rely more on factual circumstances rather than an official, legal act of registration. It is accordingly more difficult to effectuate a COMI shift for individuals. To the extent that forum shopping takes place by individuals,[16] the strategies used appear to rely more on physical movement rather than market reorientation in order to convince the court that the individual's COMI has actually shifted.

It is important to distinguish these basic strategies of COMI movement from yet another, more recent way to engage in insolvency arbitrage. Where the intended restructuring operation is not within the scope of the EIR Recast, such as the English scheme of arrangement, there is no need to actually move the COMI, because the jurisdictional tests of the Insolvency Regulation have no application to procedures falling outside its scope.[17] Such 'new' forum shopping will thus have to pass the jurisdiction tests of national law or of the Brussels I Regulation.[18] It is therefore easier to implement, and has dramatically grown in popularity over the past few years. This topic is considered separately below in Sect. 1.5.

1.3   The 2015 EIR Reform

The revised EIR Recast itself in recital 5 takes the view that '[i]t is necessary for the proper functioning of the internal market to avoid incentives for parties to transfer assets or judicial proceedings from one Member State to another, seeking to obtain a more favourable legal position to the detriment of the general body of creditors (forum shopping).' In comparison to former recital 4, the words 'to the detriment of the general body of creditors' have been added. This suggests that the revised EIR Recast seeks to differentiate between beneficial variants of forum shopping (where the 'general body' of the creditors agree) and 'fraudulent or abusive' forum shopping,[19] where the company migrates without creditors' consent or otherwise to their detriment.

---

[15] *Re Hellas Telecommunications (Luxembourg) II SCA* [2009] EWHC 3199 (Ch).

[16] Often labelled 'bankruptcy tourism'. See in detail Ringe 2016, paras 3.126 ff.

[17] *Re Rodenstock GmbH* [2011] EWHC 1104 para 54.

[18] For a recent in-depth analysis, see Mr. Justice Snowden's excellent opinion in *Re van Gansewinkel* [2015] EWHC 2151.

[19] See also recitals 29 and 31 EIR Recast: 'This Regulation should contain a number of safeguards aimed at preventing fraudulent or abusive forum shopping'.

This distinction is to be welcomed in principle; it is however not quite clear how the intellectual differentiation between different types of forum shopping translates into the new one-size-fits-all suspension period (as explained below in Sect. 1.4), for example, which does not distinguish between situations with and without creditor consent.[20] It is also unclear how the Commission comes to take the view that corporate forum shopping appears as generally beneficial, but individuals migrating for insolvency law ('bankruptcy tourism') appears to be invariably negative.[21]

In the spirit of curbing abusive forum shopping, the 2015 reform introduces a package of various measures.[22] These measures are:

i. that the COMI presumption should be rebuttable under certain circumstances;
ii. that national courts should, of their own motion, verify that the debtor's COMI is indeed located within their territory;[23]
iii. that the COMI presumption does not apply during a suspension period of three (or, in the case of individuals, six) months before the request for opening proceedings is filed; and
iv. that any creditor or debtor must have an effective remedy under national law against the decision to open insolvency proceedings.[24]

Before addressing some of the devices used in the EIR that have been designed to constrain forum shopping, a few general observations should be made. As a general matter, the revised EIR sticks to the 'COMI' principle as the primary jurisdictional connecting factor, which itself is by its very nature susceptible to manipulation, for better or worse. If the goal of the EIR revision is, as we said above, to single out those forum shopping movements that are 'abusive' or 'fraudulent', it appears that the instruments (i.), (ii.) and (iv.) listed above are modest improvements, where the judiciary is provided with further support to make assessments for each individual situation.[25] However, instrument (iii.), the suspension period, does not seem to be specifically addressed to combat only 'abusive' forum shopping situations. Rather, it makes all COMI shifting in the months before filing for insolvency more burdensome. This is an impediment also to the beneficial variants of certain COMI relocations, which would normally be value-creating for all participants.[26]

An *alternative* would have been to introduce a more radical change by abandoning the COMI concept in favour of a pure 'registered office' test for insolvency

---

[20] See below.

[21] This is the view taken in the European Commission 2012b, p. 20.

[22] See recitals 29–34 EIR Recast 2015.

[23] Article 4 EIR Recast 2015.

[24] Article 5 EIR Recast 2015.

[25] See also the assessment by de Weijs and Breeman 2014, p. 504 f.

[26] Cf. de Weijs and Breeman 2014, p. 505; Marks 2013, p. 24 (both on an earlier version of the suspension period, as proposed by the European Parliament).

jurisdiction.[27,28] This would have had the clear advantage of providing a predictable jurisdiction venue at all times and, given the relationship between choice of forum and choice of law under the EIR, a predictably applicable insolvency law. The benefits would be much reduced information costs and enhanced efficiency of any reorganisation procedure. Additionally, it would entail coherence of both company law and insolvency law, avoiding frictions between the two, since both would be equally governed by the law of the company's place of incorporation.[29]

Under such a model, forum shopping would only happen where the registered office itself (as the company's COMI) is moved from one jurisdiction to another. At the current state of EU law, only two reliable ways exist to effectuate such a cross-border relocation: using the seat transfer procedure for the *Societas Europaea*[30] or pursuing a cross-border merger under the Cross-Border Merger Directive.[31] These instruments provide for disclosure requirements and certain safeguards to be fulfilled before the cross-border operation can take place. In particular, shareholders, creditors and employees have to be adequately protected.[32] These safeguards would ensure that 'fraudulent' or 'abusive' forum shopping is effectively eliminated. Beyond these two EU-wide instruments, firms may of course want to rely on national schemes or the ECJ case-law.[33] For now, it is safe to say that these strategies do not (yet) provide for a reliable legal framework.[34]

1.4   The New Suspension Period

The main element of the new list of changes seeking to contain forum shopping is the suspension period, listed under point (iii.) above. More specifically, revised Article 3(1) provides for a suspension period to modify the registered office presumption when the debtor's COMI has been moved within a certain period prior to

---

[27] Or, of course, equating the COMI with the registered office without the availability of a rebuttal. Eidenmüller 2005, p. 447. In a similar vein, Armour 2005, p. 408.

[28] See on this and the following Ringe 2008, pp. 601 ff, 614 f and 617.

[29] For a more sceptical perspective on this concept, see Carballo Piñeiro 2014 p. 209. See also McCormack 2014, p. 49.

[30] Council Regulation (EC) No. 2157/2001 of 8 October 2001 on the Statute for a European company, [2001] OJ L294/1, Article 8. See Ringe 2007.

[31] Directive 2005/56/EC of the European Parliament and of the Council of 26 October 2005 on cross-border mergers of limited liability companies, [2005] OJ L310/1.

[32] These safeguards represent the 'price' that the company must pay in order to profit from a different (insolvency) jurisdiction. See Ringe 2007, Sect. 5.2.2.

[33] See, for example, most recently the important Polbud decision: Case C-106/16 *Polbud—Wykonawstwo sp. z o.o.* ECLI:EU:C:2017:804.

[34] This may change once the new directive is implemented into national law: See European Commission, Proposal for a Directive of the European Parliament and of The Council amending Directive (EU) 2017/1132 as regards cross-border conversions, mergers and divisions COM (2018) 241.

the filing for insolvency. In the case of companies and legal persons, the period is three months. For individuals, the time period is six months.

1.4.1 Background

The introduction of the suspension period is one of main innovations of the 2015 revision. The irony is that the European Commission, when initiating the revision process in 2012, had originally considered following a similar approach (considering even one full year), but ultimately refrained from formally proposing such a suspension period. In the view of the Commission, such an approach would not have been sufficiently effective and would have created new legal uncertainty, relating to problems in determining the exact time when a COMI is shifted.[35]

The concept of introducing a suspension period was initially proposed by INSOL Europe in its draft EIR Reform document of May 2012.[36] This proposal was for a strong suspension period of one year that would not merely disapply the operation of the presumption, but rather render any COMI shift fully ineffective for the purposes of jurisdiction under the Regulation, such that COMI would be treated as remaining in the Member State in which it had been located.[37] As the Commission's first draft refrained from picking up the idea, it was the European Parliament which urged revisiting INSOL's proposal. The European Parliament report on the EIR reform proposed introducing a genuine 'suspension' or 'neutralisation' period of three months, during which a transfer of the debtor's seat would not have altered the COMI jurisdiction.[38] This proposal did not distinguish between different types of debtor.

Later during the lawmaking process, it was the Council which for the first time proposed different COMI presumption rules for different types of debtor; only individuals not engaged in exercising an independent business or professional activity were subject to a six-month suspension period.[39] During the ensuing trilogue negotiations, both institutions agreed on the present approach.[40]

---

[35] European Commission 2012b, p. 35; European Parliament 2013, p. 4.

[36] INSOL Europe 2012, p. 38 ff.

[37] INSOL also proposed exceptions to the rule, for example where the creditors consented to the COMI shift. See INSOL Europe 2012, p. 39.

[38] European Parliament, Committee on Legal Affairs 2013. See Latella 2014, p. 489.

[39] 'General Approach': Council document 10284/14 ADD 1 (3 June 2014) 10.

[40] Council, Outcomes of the first trilogue held on 15 October 2014, Document 14462/14.

1.4.2 Context

A number of jurisdictions have a similar suspension rule in their domestic insolvency law. French insolvency law, for instance, does not recognise a transfer of the COMI if this change took place within six months before the application for insolvency proceedings.[41] Similar provisions are in force in Spain[42] and Italy.[43] Even the draft EC Insolvency Convention from 1980 (one of the precursors to the enactment of the EIR) contained a specific provision for the event of a cross-border transfer of the debtor's registered office, according to which the courts of the former state would retain jurisdiction for a transitional period of six months.[44] The objective of all of these rules is to discourage pre-filing forum shopping, on an assumption that the temporal proximity of the COMI transfer to the filing for insolvency is an indicator of a fraudulent or abusive purpose.

1.4.3 Operation

The suspension period under the recast EIR is triggered where the registered office has been moved across borders within a period of three months before the debtor company files for insolvency. If this is the case, the presumption (according to which the registered office corresponds to the COMI) is irrelevant and should not be applied. As a consequence, the court seised with the proceedings needs to establish the (real) COMI on the basic COMI definition alone and may not rely on the presumption that is specified in EIR Article 3(1). This rule can be understood as a 'weak' variant of a suspension period, in that it only disapplies the COMI presumption, rather than treating any potential COMI shift as entirely ineffective for the purposes of the jurisdictional rules of the Regulation.[45]

---

[41] Circulaire de la DACS n° 2006–19 du 15 décembre 2006 relative au règlement n° 1346/2000 du 29 mai 2000 relatif aux procédures d'insolvabilité, para 1.2.1.; Jazottes and Monsèrié-Bon 2007, para 12.

[42] Marshall, para 1.007.

[43] Frind 2008, p. 365.

[44] See Article 6 Draft Convention on bankruptcy, winding-up, arrangements, compositions and similar proceedings 1980, EC Bulletin Supplement 2/82, available at http://aei.pitt.edu/5480/.

[45] In this way, it needs to be distinguished from a 'hard' suspension, as proposed by the European Parliament, see above n 36. In favour of a hard suspension period: Carballo Piñeiro 2014, p. 210.

1.4.4 Critique

The new suspension period in the EIR is confronted with some severe criticisms. First, it may be *under-inclusive*. It is important to note that the suspension period does not apply if it is only the company's head office which has been moved to another Member State (without the registered office): this follows from the explicit wording of the provision, which only refers to situations where 'the registered has [...] been moved to another Member State'. As we saw above, however, simply moving the head office or central administration of a company is a common way of forum shopping.[46] It is submitted that these situations can equally lead to forum shopping, and that the provision thus exposes a serious gap.

At the same time, however, the provision risks being *over-inclusive*: it may discourage even beneficial forum shifts that are agreed between the debtor and all creditors.[47] As the present author argued elsewhere, forum shopping may be beneficial where all concerned parties (in particular, the creditors) agree to it.[48] Where mutual agreement is missing, potential disadvantages for creditors may be mitigated by means of specific creditor protection laws or other safeguards.[49] The point, however, is that the new suspension period does not distinguish between whether a COMI shift was carried out in mutual agreement (which would be beneficial) or as a unilateral decision by the debtor. It is only the latter that regulatory attempts should target.

Fixing a three months period may, in addition, turn out to be easily susceptible to manipulation, particularly given that there may well be uncertainty as to the precise moment the COMI was moved.[50] The COMI is defined by a reference to a set of facts and activities (e.g. administration activities) and a transfer of these activities from one Member State to another does not always take place overnight. Practitioners report that a COMI migration often takes between six and twelve weeks.[51] The period of three months also appears arbitrary and has not been justified by any substantial reasons.[52]

Further, disapplying the presumption gives preference to the debtor's previous COMI. That however may in some situations prove unfair to new creditors, that is

---

[46] See above Sect. 1.2.

[47] See above Sect. 1.3.

[48] Ringe 2008, pp. 600 ff.

[49] Ringe 2008, pp. 600 ff.

[50] The Commission had this concern itself. See European Commission 2012b, p. 35; European Parliament 2013, p. 4. See also the UK Delegation, Comments on the Commission Proposal, Council Document 9080/13, p. 3: '[A suspension period] creates an unnecessary complication to the procedure for determining jurisdiction and reduces, rather than increases, legal certainty for stakeholders.'

[51] McGovern and Hatchard 2015.

[52] Marks 2013, p. 24 (on the planned one year suspension period).

to say creditors who acquired their claims against the debtor *after* the COMI shift had been effected.[53] Those new creditors will not normally be aware of the former location of the COMI of their debtor. Neither do they usually know the exact date when the COMI was shifted. Thus, the opening of insolvency proceedings in the Member State where the COMI was formerly located may be unforeseeable to them. Generally, the risk of relocation of the COMI should be borne by the former creditors, not by new ones (former creditors are cheaper risk avoiders, i.e. they are generally better at bearing the risk).

An entirely different problem is that the suspension period could prove to be without real effect. The reason lies in the way the suspension period is drafted in the EIR Recast, which requires nothing more than the disapplication of the 'registered office presumption'. This, by itself, does not make COMI shifts impossible. On the contrary, as seen above, the performance of head office functions can be moved while leaving behind the registered office; alternatively, both registered office and head office functions may be moved to another Member State, followed by an immediate filing for insolvency: and the courts in the new Member State may still be convinced that the new COMI is within their jurisdiction. As others have observed, the use of a weaker form of suspension period that merely disapplies the presumption means that genuine COMI shifts can still be achieved.[54]

Finally, the suspension period is problematic with regard to a potential conflict with the freedom of establishment. As one of the four freedoms, establishment is a cornerstone of the EU internal market. It allows individuals and companies or firms[55] to 'establish' themselves in another Member State, that is, to 'participate, on a stable and continuous basis, in the economic life of a Member State other than [their] State of origin and to profit therefrom'.[56] Breaches of this principle can only be justified in exceptional circumstances.[57] Against this backdrop, restricting the possibilities of moving the COMI could represent an unjustified restriction of establishment.[58]

To be sure, some of these concerns are mitigated by the fact that the suspension period in the form adopted by the EIR Recast 2015 is only a 'soft' form of a suspension period. The lawmakers refrained from adopting a 'hard' suspension

---

[53] Garcimartín, p. 6.

[54] House of Commons, Select Committee, European Scrutiny Committee, debate on 26 November 2014 ('Insolvency Proceedings'): 'We do not believe this change will impact adversely on genuine COMI relocation cases as the court is not prevented from finding COMI without the ability to rely on the presumptions under Article 3(1). This maintains a definition of the centre of main interest that is based on commercial reality.' Available at http://www.publications. parliament.uk/pa/cm201415/cmselect/cmeuleg/219-xxi/21913.htm.

[55] For companies and firms, see Article 54 TFEU.

[56] Case C-55/94 *Reinhard Gebhard v Consiglio dell'Ordine degli Avvocati e Procuratori di Milano*, [1995] ECR I-4165, ECLI:EU:C:1995:411, para 25.

[57] Article 52 TFEU.

[58] The Commission notes the tension with the freedom of establishment in European Commission 2012b, p. 20. See also Hess 2013; UK Delegation (n 50), p. 3.

period, where the existence of the COMI in a newly chosen Member State is fully rejected during a certain period. Instead, the only thing the suspension period does it to disapply the presumption. That is, the court of the newly chosen Member State may, even within the suspension period, come to the view that the COMI has genuinely been relocated to the new venue of choice.

In sum, the suspension period is an inappropriate tool to address abusive forum shopping. In particular, it does not live up to the (otherwise, laudable) goal of curbing abusive versions of forum shopping while maintaining beneficial COMI shifts. We shall now consider alternative concepts to achieve this.

1.4.5   Alternative Mechanisms

From a perspective of legal policy, there are alternative mechanisms to respond to pre-filing shifts. This assumes, of course, that such shifts need to be regulated at all. As discussed above, there is much to be said for allowing COMI movements as long as either (i) all constituents agree or (ii) adequate safeguards exist for those who disagree.

If, however, a specific anti-forum shopping rule is to be designed, a more targeted rule should have been and should be considered. For example, in its original proposal, INSOL Europe allowed for an exception from the look-back period it proposed (similar to a suspension period) for the case where all creditors have agreed to the COMI shift.[59] Further, during the legislative negotiations on the EIR revision, the delegations from the Netherlands, Germany and Spain proposed an alternative, more abuse-specific test.[60] According to this proposal, any transfer of the COMI would have to be disregarded whenever its 'exclusive or main object or effect was to harm the interests of creditors or employees'.[61] In addition, the proposal suggested supporting this principle by a presumption that 'Subject to proof to the contrary by the debtor, a transfer of the COMI is in particular deemed to harm the interests of creditors or employees when: a. the transfer occurred at a time when the debtor was already insolvent, or b. the request for the opening of insolvency proceedings was made within [three] months of the transfer of the COMI.'[62]

These alternative approaches would have had several advantages. First, the INSOL proposal would have allowed for flexibility where all creditors consent, which would be an indicator for beneficial forum shopping.[63] Secondly, also the Dutch/German/Spanish proposal would have been more specifically addressed to

---

[59] INSOL Europe 2012, p. 39 [proposed Article 3(1)(i)].

[60] *Proposals from the delegations of the Netherlands, Germany and Spain on abusive COMI-transfer*, Council document 10306/14 (10 June 2014).

[61] Ibid. 3.

[62] Ibid. 4.

[63] See above n 37.

the 'abuse' problem, in line with the overall objective to target only 'abusive' or 'fraudulent' forum shopping, and not beneficial COMI shifts. Thirdly, both proposals would have used a different strategy of disregarding the COMI shift itself, not just the COMI presumption, as seen above. This would be the more straightforward and direct form of suspension period.

The Dutch/German/Spanish solution would have also been more in line with domestic responses in the national case law in Germany and the UK. Unlike France and other Member States, German law does not provide for a suspension rule, but courts have been suspicious about migration in the vicinity of insolvency all the same. In a case from 1996, the Federal Supreme Court said in *obiter dictum* that an application for insolvency within three weeks of the migration would constitute abusive behaviour and would normally be disregarded.[64]

English domestic law is interpreted in such a way that a person who has carried on business in England is treated as continuing the business for the purposes of bankruptcy jurisdiction until he has made arrangements to settle his business debts.[65] Similarly, in *TXU*,[66] an English registrar accepted that forum shopping could undermine creditors' rights and implied that he might not have granted the order sought in the event the debtor's recent cross-border migration had caused prejudice to foreign creditors.

Academic comment has discussed a range of solutions for tackling cross-border migration problems. Some authors suggest that in extreme cases, decisions could be rejected on the grounds of *ordre public*[67] or *abuse of law*.[68] Others argue for a broad interpretation of the 'applicable law' under Article 7 of the Regulation in order to give debtors no incentive to engage in forum shopping.[69] Still others advocate for a criterion of 'permanence' for the interpretation of the COMI.[70] And finally, some authors even suggest amending the Regulation in a way that would make it unambiguously clear that forum shopping is not allowed under the Regulation.[71]

Each of these proposals has its advantages and inherent problems. It seems important to introduce most of all some degree of flexibility into the system. Bearing in mind the distinction made above between beneficial and detrimental variants of forum shopping, it appears paramount to give courts some degree of discretion to distinguish the former from the latter. The hard three months period does not appear to fit into this line of thinking.

---

[64] Bundesgerichtshof, judgment of 20 March 1996, X ARZ 90/96, reported in BGHZ 132, 195.

[65] *Re A Debtor (No. 784 of 1991)* [1992] Ch. 554; *Theophile v Solicitor-General* [1950] AC 186 (HL); see Moss et al. 2009, para 8.105.

[66] *Re TXU Europe German Finance BV* [2005] BCC 90 para 19.

[67] Rotstegge 2008, p. 961.

[68] Eidenmüller 2011.

[69] Kindler 2018, para 5.

[70] Jazottes and Monsèrié-Bon 2007; Frind 2008, p. 365. See also Weller 2004, p. 416.

[71] Moss and Paulus 2006, p. 3.

1.5   Forum Shopping Beyond the EIR Recast,
and 'Schemes of Arrangement'

A more recent trend of insolvency arbitrage relates to forum shopping 'outside' of
the EIR's Recast scope. Restructuring proceedings that do not come within the
scope of application of the EIR Recast by virtue of appendix A do not fall under the
Regulation's rules concerning jurisdiction (Articles 3 ff) and applicable law
(Articles 7 ff). Member States are therefore free to individually determine the
jurisdictional framework for such proceedings, and may in particular greatly
facilitate access to them.

This development has been particularly evident in use of the 'scheme of
arrangement', a restructuring mechanism under English law which is governed by
Sections 895 ff of the Companies Act 2006. The scheme of arrangement is a statutory
process which allows the company to enter into agreements with its members and/or
creditors to reach an unlimited variety of restructuring operations.[72] The scheme is
characterised by a strong role of the court: any scheme agreed by the parties must be
sanctioned by the court. As a *quid pro quo*, the scheme of arrangement has the great
advantage that it allows a majority of the shareholders or creditors to bind the
minority; this includes secured creditors, provided that creditor classes are properly
constituted. If a 'majority in number representing 75% in value' of the creditors or
shareholders (as the case may be) vote in favour of the scheme, and the scheme is
subsequently sanctioned by the court, the scheme will be binding on the dissenting
minority, unless fraud can be demonstrated.

This attractive restructuring mechanism has attracted a great number of foreign
companies in recent years, mostly due to the fact that many continental jurisdictions
do not offer a comparably effective procedure. At the same time, English courts
have been ready to open up the scope of eligible companies that may make use of
the scheme.[73] Thus, English courts as a general matter have jurisdiction to sanction
schemes involving foreign companies, although the court will not exercise its
jurisdiction unless 'sufficient connection with England' is shown. What is considered to be a sufficient connection with England for this purpose has become more
settled over time, although, of course, this is a fact-sensitive issue.[74]

In practice, the most common situation is that English law as the governing law
for the creditor arrangements (and a jurisdiction clause in favour of UK courts)
provides a sufficient connection to England and is considered as satisfying the

---

[72] For a comprehensive overview, see O'Dea et al. 2012; Payne 2014; Bryant 2011.

[73] For example, *Re Drax Holdings Ltd* [2004] 1 WLR 1049; *Trimast Holding Sarl v
TeleColumbus GmbH* [2010] EWHC 1944 (Ch); *Re Rodenstock GmbH* [2011] EWHC 1104.

[74] Seelinger and Daehnert 2012; Lowe 2014.

scheme jurisdiction.[75] In a recent case, where the creditor claims were not subject to English law, the courts have even endorsed a comprehensive transaction where the parties first changed the applicable law from German to English law and then carried out a scheme of arrangement.[76] In yet another line of cases, where neither the company's registered office was in the UK, nor the debt was subject to English law, the courts can nevertheless sanction a scheme where the COMI of the debtor is or has been shifted to the UK.[77]

The permissibility of a scheme from the perspective of the English courts needs to be distinguished from whether the scheme can later be enforced in the jurisdiction where the scheme company is domiciled.[78] This question is often overlooked, but seems to be a major issue determining the overall attractiveness of the scheme.[79] Continental jurisdictions struggle with a doctrinal answer to the question, partly because the scheme does not fit into any of the established categories of civil procedure known on the continent, and indeed the scheme falls somewhere between a collective and an individual procedure. This causes some confusion as to whether either the EIR Recast, the Brussels I Regulation or neither of them is applicable to determine jurisdiction and recognition.[80]

In one case, the German Federal Supreme Court rejected the recognition of an English scheme for a German company, but it is possible that the outcome of this decision is due to the specific framework for insurance companies and might not be transferable to other types of companies.[81] In fact, most other (lower instance) courts have been rather pragmatic and mostly accepted recognition of English schemes, using different doctrinal paths.[82] US courts have recognised a scheme under Chapter 15 of the US Bankruptcy Code.[83]

---

[75] *Re Rodenstock GmbH* [2011] EWHC 1104; *Primacom Holding GmbH & another v A Group of Senior Lenders & Credit Agricole* [2011] EWHC 3746 (Ch); *Primacom Holding GmbH & another v A Group of Senior Lenders & Credit Agricole* [2012] EWHC 164 (Ch); *Cortefiel SA and MEP 11 Sarl* [2012] EWHC 2998 (Ch); *Re Vietnam Shipbuilding Industry Group* [2013] EWHC 2476 (Ch).

[76] *Apcoa Parking (UK) Ltd* [2014] EWHC 997 (Ch) and [2014] EWHC 1897 (Ch). See also *Re DTEK Finance BV* [2015] EWHC 1164 (Ch).

[77] *Re Magyar Telecom BV* [2013] EWHC 3800 (Ch); *Re Zlomrex International Finance SA* [2013] EWHC 4605 (Ch).

[78] In fact, the English courts assess the future enforceability before they endorse the scheme in each individual case, but they appear rather generous with this requirement.

[79] And in fact, a legal barrier ex ante: *Sompo Japan Insurance Inc v Transfercom Ltd* [2007] EWHC 146 (Ch), *Re Rodenstock GmbH* at [73]–[77].

[80] For a recent overview of the question, see *Re van Gansewinkel* [2015] EWHC 2151. For comment, see Bork 2013; Kuipers 2012.

[81] Bundesgerichtshof, decision of 15 February 2012 (IV ZR 194/09), [2012] NJW 2113 (*Equitable Life*).

[82] Recognising the scheme, for example, Landgericht (Regional Court) Rottweil, decision of 17 May 2010 (3 O 2/08), [2010] ZIP 1964; rejecting it, by contrast, OLG (Court of Appeal) Celle, decision of 8 September 2009 (8 U 46/09), [2009] ZIP 1968.

[83] *In re Magyar Telecom B.V.*, Case No. 13-13508 (SHL) (Bankr. D. Del. Dec. 12, 2013).

For the present purpose, it is important to note that such cases of 'scheme' forum shopping do not fall within the scope of the EIR Recast and are therefore not subject to the jurisdiction requirements laid down in Article 3.[84] In the run-up to the 2015 reform, when policy-makers sought to extend the Regulation's scope, the UK government insisted that schemes of arrangement should not be covered by the EIR Recast.[85] They were successful with this demand, and new recital 16 clarifies that 'proceedings that are based on general company law not designed exclusively for insolvency situations should not be considered to be based on laws relating to insolvency' and hence not within the scope of the EIR Recast. Offering such a restructuring mechanism to foreign companies unrestrained by the EIR Recast appears to be an important source of revenue for the UK restructuring business and law firms.

Is unrestricted shopping for a scheme of arrangement desirable? We should follow the same logic as above: offering choice for restructuring procedures may be beneficial if either all parties agree or if adequate safeguards exist for those who disagree. The scheme of arrangement benefits from a strict court control to safe-guard the interests of dissenting minorities and would as such effectively respond to the risk of opportunism. Nevertheless, a number of improvements would be desirable. First, it would be helpful to have a clearer criterion for when English courts have jurisdiction, as the current regime seems rather broad and somewhat arbitrary. Secondly, significant expansions of the scheme's scope, such by an ex post change of the applicable law governing the loan agreements[86] should only apply for future creditors who are then able to price in the risk adequately, and not retroactively. Finally, the question of recognition of a scheme in some other jurisdictions is still unresolved.

1.6 Conclusion

This chapter has demonstrated the inherent flaws of the new regime governing insolvency arbitrage in the European Union. The 2015 reform starts from the sensible proposition to distinguish between beneficial and 'abusive' variants of forum shopping. However, the key element of the reform, the introduction of a three-month suspension period, is over-inclusive in applying to all pre-filing COMI shifts. At the same time, the new rule is also under-inclusive in not applying to situations where only the company's head office is moved to a new jurisdiction. At best, the new rule may be entirely without effect due to its application to the

---

[84] *Re van Gansewinkel* [2015] EWHC 2151 para 4.

[85] The European Commission had initially considered covering schemes of arrangement. See European Commssion 2012c, p. 6. The UK's lobbying efforts were successful to keep schemes of arrangement outside the scope of the EIR to 'preserve the UK's restructuring flexibility and the use of schemes in both the corporate and restructuring context'. See Tett and Crinson 2015, p. 66.

[86] As in *Apcoa Parking (UK) Ltd* [2014] EWHC 997 (Ch) and [2014] EWHC 1897 (Ch).

'presumption' aspect of the COMI only. But even then, the new rule will create significant uncertainty and undermine effective ways of business restructuring.

At the same time, the reform does not address new variants of forum shopping outside of the EIR's Recast scope, such as the use of the English scheme of arrangement by continental European firms. Such 'procedural' forum shopping may be effected entirely without COMI relocation at all, as it does not come within the scope of application of the EIR Recast. The UK was successful in convincing lawmakers that it should remain outside of the EIR Recast and therefore continues to be free to set the criteria for the scheme's application independent from Brussels. As much as choice of a restructuring mechanism is desirable, the current regime governing schemes should have been clarified and strengthened.

The laudable goal of the EIR Recast to improve the pricing of risks in cross-border insolvencies is jeopardised where the rules on jurisdiction are unclear or uncertain. The 2015 EIR reform is a missed opportunity to improve the system by attaching insolvency law and jurisdiction to a company's registered office as the only clear and predictable connecting factor. Instead, the reform introduces new riddles and inconsistencies. Such steps will blur rather than improve the pricing of insolvency risk and thereby ultimately drive up the cost of capital.

References

Armour J (2005) Who Should Make Corporate Law? EC Legislation versus Regulatory Competition. Current Legal Problems 58:369

Bork R (2013) Zur Frage der Anerkennung eines gerichtlich genehmigten Vergleichsplans nach englischem Gesellschaftsrecht – einem 'Scheme of Arrangement'. Zeitschrift für Europäisches Privatrecht (ZEuP) 136

Bork R, van Zwieten K (2016) Commentary on the European Insolvency Regulation. Oxford University Press, Oxford

Bryant C (2011) Schemes of Arrangement. In: Prentice D, Reisberg A (eds) Corporate Finance Law in the UK and EU. Oxford University Press, Oxford, 59

Carballo Piñeiro L (2014) Towards the reform of the European Insolvency Regulation: codification rather than modification. Nederlands Internationaal Privaatrecht (NIPR) 207

de Weijs RJ, Breeman MS (2014) Comi-migration: Use or Abuse of European Insolvency Law? European Company and Financial Law Review 11:479

Eidenmüller H (2011) Abuse of Law in the context of European Insolvency Law. In: de la Feria R, Vogenauer S (eds) Prohibition of Abuse of Law: A New General Principle of EU Law? Hart Publishing, Oxford, pp 137

Eidenmüller H (2005) Free Choice in International Company Insolvency Law in Europe. EBOR 6:423

European Commission (2012a) Proposal for a Regulation of the European Parliament and of the Council amending Council Regulation (EC) No. 1346/2000 on insolvency proceedings, COM (2012) 744 (12 December 2012)

European Commission (2012b) Impact Assessment accompanying the Revision Proposal, SWD (2012) 416 final (12 December 2012)

European Commission (2012c) Report to the European Parliament, the Council and the European Economic and Social Committee on the application of Council Regulation (EC) No. 1346/2000 of 29 May 2000 on insolvency proceedings, COM(2012) 743 final

European Parliament (2011) Report with recommendations to the Commission on insolvency proceedings in the context of EU company law (2011/2006(INI)), Committee on Legal Affairs ('Lehne Report')

European Parliament (2013) Initial appraisal of a European Commission Impact Assessment – European Commission proposal for a Regulation on insolvency proceedings

European Parliament Committee on Legal Affairs (2013) Report on the proposal for a regulation of the European Parliament and of the Council amending Council Regulation (EC) No. 1346/2000 on insolvency proceedings (20 December 2013), Document A7-0481/2013

Frind F (2008) Forum PINning? Zeitschrift für das gesamte Insolvenzrecht (ZInsO) 11:363

Garcimartín F (undated) The EU Insolvency Regulation: Rules on Jurisdiction, http://www.ejtn.eu/PageFiles/6333/Rules_on_jurisdiction.pdf accessed 21 June 2019

Hess B (2013) Jurisdiction. In: Heidelberg-Vienna-Luxembourg Report on the Application of Regulation No. 1346/2000/EC on Insolvency Proceedings (External Evaluation JUST/2011/JCIV/PR/0049/A4), https://www.mpi.lu/uploads/media/evaluation_insolvency_en.pdf accessed 21 June 2019

INSOL Europe (2012) Revision of the European Insolvency Regulation

Jazottes G, Monsèrié-Bon MH (2007) Premières applications du règlement insolvabilité: la recherche de l'efficacité. Revue Europe 8, étude 19

Kindler P (2018) Art. 7 EuInsVO. In: Münchener Kommentar zum BGB, 7th edn. CH Beck, Munich

Kuipers JJ (2012) Schemes of Arrangement and Voluntary Collective Redress: A Gap In The Brussels I Regulation. Journal of Private International Law 8:225

Latella D (2014) The 'COMI' Concept in the Revision of the European Insolvency Regulation. European Company and Financial Law Review 11:479

Lowe R (2014) The Rise and Rise of Schemes. Insolvency Intelligence 27:32

Marks D (2013) European Insolvency Regulation: Where Does It Go Next? International Corporate Rescue 10:22

Marshall J (ed) (undated) European Cross Border Insolvency (loose-leaf publication). Sweet & Maxwell, London

McCormack G (2009) Jurisdictional Competition and Forum Shopping in Insolvency Proceedings. Cambridge Law Journal 68:169

McCormack G (2010) Reconstructing European insolvency law – putting in place a new paradigm. Legal Studies 30:126

McCormack G (2014) Reforming the European Insolvency Regulation: A Legal and Policy Perspective. Journal of Private International Law 10:41

McGovern EA, Hatchard J (2015) Forum shopping – the end of an era? Global Restructuring Watch (29 May 2015), http://www.globalrestructuringwatch.com/2015/05/forum-shopping-the-end-of-an-era/, accessed 31 January 2019

Mevorach I (2013) Forum Shopping in Times of Crisis: A Directors' Duties Perspective. European Company and Financial Law Review 10:523

Moss G, Fletcher I, Isaacs S (2009) The EC Regulation on Insolvency Proceedings: A Commentary and Annotated Guide, 2nd edn. Oxford University Press, Oxford

Moss G, Paulus C (2006) The European Insolvency Regulation – The Case for Urgent Reform. Insolvency Intelligence 19:1

O'Dea G, Long J, Smyth A (2012) Schemes of Arrangement: Law and Practice. Oxford University Press, Oxford

Payne J (2014) Schemes of Arrangement: Theory, Structure and Operation. Cambridge University Press, Cambridge

Ringe WG (2007) The European Company Statute in the Context of Freedom of Establishment. Journal of Corporate Law Studies 7:185–212

Ringe WG (2008) Forum Shopping under the EU Insolvency Regulation. EBOR 9:579

Ringe WG (2016) Article 3. In: Bork R, van Zwieten K (eds) Commentary on the European Insolvency Regulation. Oxford University Press, Oxford

Rotstegge JP (2008) Zuständigkeitsfragen bei der Insolvenz in- und ausländischer Konzerngesellschaften. Zeitschrift für Wirtschaftsrecht 955

Seelinger J, Daehnert A (2012) International Jurisdiction for Schemes of Arrangement. International Corporate Rescue 9:243

Tett R, Crinson K (2015) The recast EC Regulation on Insolvency Proceedings: a welcome revision. Corporate Rescue and Insolvency 8:64

Weller MP (2004) Forum Shopping im Internationalen Insolvenzrecht? Praxis des Internationalen Privat- und Verfahrensrechts (IPRax) 24:412

Chapter 2
Contracting Around Insolvency Jurisdiction: Private Ordering in European Insolvency Jurisdiction Rules and Practices

Ilya Kokorin

Contents

Abstract Insolvency law is driven by various policy considerations. This is why, as opposed to the domain of contract law, the room for private regulation in insolvency has always been limited. The 'choice' of an insolvency jurisdiction is not an exception. Since the adoption of the first European Insolvency Regulation (EIR) in 2000, determination of the international insolvency forum has been determined by the presence of the debtor's centre of main interests (COMI). In the EIR of 2015, COMI is defined as 'the place where the debtor conducts the administration of its interests on a regular basis and which is ascertainable by third parties.' Conceptually, COMI cannot be controlled or chosen by the parties (debtors

I. Kokorin (✉)
Department of Financial Law, Leiden Law School, Steenschuur 25,
2311 ES Leiden, The Netherlands
e-mail: i.kokorin@law.leidenuniv.nl

© T.M.C. ASSER PRESS and the authors 2020
V. Lazić and S. Stuij (eds.), *Recasting the Insolvency Regulation*, Short Studies in Private International Law,
https://doi.org/10.1007/978-94-6265-363-4_2

and creditors). This chapter argues that there are situations in which COMI fails to make international insolvency jurisdiction ascertainable or efficient. These include investment in capital markets, groups of companies, decentralised management and platform-based business models. The changing commercial environment in which companies operate, the rising power of (certain groups of) creditors and the thrust towards rescuing ailing companies have led to the emergence of different mechanisms of private nature that allow (partial) regulation of the insolvency process. This chapter attempts to make sense of this development and explore whether a conceivable shift to a contractual paradigm in insolvency has manifested itself in insolvency jurisdiction rules and practices in Europe. Such exploration will involve the analysis of a contractual COMI-choice, synthetic/reverse synthetic insolvency proceedings and the selection of a group coordination forum.

Keywords Insolvency · Centre of main interests (COMI) · Forum selection · Synthetic insolvency proceedings · Corporate groups · Decentralised management · European Insolvency Regulation

2.1 Introduction

The value of ascertainability of the insolvency forum (insolvency jurisdiction) is hard to overestimate. This forum determines whether insolvency proceedings can be commenced, and in case the court of the forum assumes jurisdiction, the law of such a forum will usually govern the effects of the opening of insolvency proceedings and such issues, as ranking of claims, distribution of proceeds, transaction avoidance and directors' liability. In addition to legal implications, the 'selection' of an insolvency jurisdiction influences the amount of costs related to administration of insolvency proceedings and participation of creditors in them. This is why legal certainty is crucial for creditors, as they need to calculate investment-related risks and risk premiums built into investment beforehand.

Since the adoption of the European Insolvency Regulation in 2000 (EIR),[1] the concept of 'centre of main interests' (COMI) has played a leading role in allocating international jurisdiction in cross-border insolvency cases within the European Union (EU). The importance of COMI comes from the fact that it determines which court has jurisdiction to handle debtor's insolvency and which law will govern insolvency proceedings. The new Insolvency Regulation,[2] in force since 26 June 2017 (EIR Recast), stipulates that COMI 'shall be the place where the debtor conducts the administration of its interests on a regular basis and which is ascertainable by third parties' (Article 3(1) EIR Recast).

---

[1] Council Regulation (EC) No. 1346/2000 of 29 May 2000 on insolvency proceedings.

[2] Regulation (EU) 2015/848 of the European Parliament and of the Council of 20 May 2015 on insolvency proceedings (recast).

Despite the decisive role of the COMI concept, since its introduction in the EIR, the determination of a centre of main interests has been tainted by uncertainty and has become a matter for protracted litigation. This chapter offers a critique of the existing (European) doctrine of international insolvency jurisdiction. There are three major reasons for this. The first comes from the inherent vagueness and fluidity of the concept. The second one relates to the scenario of corporate group insolvency, addressed in the newly established Chap. 5 EIR Recast. Despite the apparent progress made in this area, group centralisation for the purposes of efficient and effective debt resolution remains hindered by the prevailing entity-by-entity approach. The third reason comes from the changing nature of businesses and their underlying organisational structures over the last two decades. For instance, platform-based enterprises and decentralised autonomous organisations make it difficult (if not impossible) to pinpoint a particular jurisdiction of the debtor's 'nerve centre'.[3] Indeed, the very criterion of a place where the debtor 'conducts the administration of its interests' loses its salience when such a place cannot be identified with reasonable certainty.

This chapter is an attempt to restart the discussion on the rules determining insolvency forum and the role salient stakeholders, such as creditors and debtors, have in selecting it. It begins with a brief outline of the concept of COMI and its current mode of operation (Sect. 2.2). Then it reviews a selection of bond prospectuses, issued by companies wishing to raise capital across the EU securities markets, to probe the expectations the bondholders have (or should be considered as having) in a case of the issuer's insolvency, particularly in terms of the insolvency forum, applicable law and the restructuring regime (Sect. 2.3.1). The difficulties of applying the COMI-standard are studied in the context of multinational enterprise groups (Sect. 2.3.2) and emerging platform-based and decentralised business models (Sect. 2.3.3). While Sect. 2.3 uncovers shortcomings of the current European insolvency model and its weaknesses in the face of modern developments, Sect. 2.4 addresses potential ways of improving predictability and effectiveness of rules on international insolvency jurisdiction.

The changing business environment in which companies operate, the rising power of (certain groups of) creditors and the thrust towards rescuing ailing companies have led to the emergence of various mechanisms of private nature that allow (partial) regulation of the insolvency process. This chapter attempts to make sense of this development and explore whether a conceivable shift to a contractual paradigm in insolvency has manifested itself in insolvency jurisdiction rules and practices in Europe. This exploration involves the review of instances of contractual insolvency forum selection (Sect. 2.4.1), the analysis of synthetic/reverse synthetic insolvency proceedings (Sect. 2.4.2) and a brief introduction to the choice of a group coordination forum (Sect. 2.4.3).

---

[3] 'Nerve center' has been described as the 'principal place of business [...] from which a corporation radiates out to its constituent parts and from which its officers direct, control and coordinate all activities.' *Phoenix Four v. Strategic Resources Corp.*, 446 F.Supp.2d 205, 214–215 (S.D.N.Y. 2006). See also Wessels 2015, para 10236a.

Based on recent case law and legal developments, it is argued that there may be a room for the use of private arrangements to constructing (contracting around) insolvency jurisdiction. Such arrangements seem to be more welcome as an *ex post* strategy, a strategy pursued upon the initiation of insolvency proceedings. *Ex ante* contracting in insolvency remains marginal but can still increase insolvency-related predictability and efficient risk allocation, thus empowering private parties (insolvency stakeholders) to engineer their own fate.

2.2 International Insolvency Jurisdiction and Centre of Main Interests

The idea of devising a connecting factor for insolvency proceedings is not new. If properly implemented, this factor should indicate to the debtor's creditors and other stakeholders the jurisdiction where the insolvency proceedings can be started, as well as the law applicable to the debtor's insolvency. The concept of COMI was designed to serve as such connecting factor. In insolvency and restructuring matters, its origin can be traced to the 1980 Draft Convention on Bankruptcy, Winding-Up, Arrangements, Compositions and Similar Proceedings[4] (1980 Draft Convention).

The 1980 Draft Convention was one of the early attempts to harmonise insolvency-related jurisdictional rules in the European Economic Community (EEC). It took a strong pro-unity (one debtor, one insolvency proceeding) stance and proposed a term 'centre of administration', decisive in determining international jurisdiction. It reads in Article 3(1): 'Where the centre of administration of the debtor is situated in one of the Contracting States, the courts of that State shall have exclusive jurisdiction to declare the debtor bankrupt.' According to Article 3(2), the centre of administration meant the place where the debtor usually administers its main interests. Due to proposed exclusivity, countries not having the debtor's 'centre of administration' were precluded from opening parallel insolvency proceedings.[5] However, local interests remained protected by the application of national insolvency rules with respect to assets located in each EEC jurisdiction.[6]

---

[4] Draft Convention on bankruptcy, winding-up, arrangements, compositions and similar proceedings. Report on the draft Convention. Bulletin of the European Communities, Supplement 2/82 (1982), http://aei.pitt.edu/5480/1/5480.pdf. Accessed 1 June 2019.

[5] States were allowed to open insolvency proceedings in the absence of 'centre of administration' only when (1) such centre was not in a Contracting State and (2) the debtor had an establishment in a Contracting State, requested to open insolvency proceedings (Article 4(1) 1980 Convention).

[6] As a consequence, multiplicity of insolvency estates (sub-estates) was created. This approach was inherited from the EEC Preliminary Draft Convention on Bankruptcy, Winding-up, Arrangements, Compositions, and Similar Proceedings (1970). The approach, if adopted, would have led to a perplexing and cumbersome arrangement. According to Fletcher, '[t]he sheer complexity of the exercise was truly horrifying, and would have resulted in much wasteful expenditure of administrative resources.' Fletcher 2016, para 1.17.

Despite the fact that the 1980 Convention was not adopted, the idea of having a connecting jurisdictional link in international insolvency cases migrated to the 1990 Istanbul Convention,[7] drafted under the auspices of the Council of Europe. It then reappeared in the 1995 European Convention on Insolvency Proceedings (1995 Convention), a document which strongly influenced both the UNCITRAL Model Law on Cross-Border Insolvency of 1997 (Model Law) and the EIR (now recast).[8] The 1995 Convention and the authoritative report accompanying it, the Virgós-Schmit Report,[9] proposed a model in which main insolvency proceedings having a universal scope were linked to (could be opened at) the jurisdiction of the debtor's COMI. The same approach is now followed by the EIR Recast.

The EIR Recast is the major instrument regulating cross-border insolvencies in the EU and is directly applicable in all EU Member States (except Denmark), replacing domestic private international law rules.[10] According to Article 3(1) EIR Recast, 'centre of main interests' is defined as a place where the debtor 'conducts the administration of its interests on a regular basis and which is ascertainable by third parties.' In case of a legal entity, the place of the registered office is presumed to be the centre of its main interests in the absence of proof to the contrary. COMI performs two main functions within the system of the EIR Recast. Firstly, it allocates international insolvency jurisdiction for the opening of main insolvency proceedings. Secondly, COMI-jurisdiction usually determines the law applicable to insolvency proceedings (*lex concursus*), their effects on rights and duties of a debtor and its creditors. For example, *lex concursus* governs powers of the debtor and insolvency practitioners, rules governing the distribution of proceeds from the realisation of assets and ranking of claims (see Article 7 EIR Recast). In addition to legal implications, the 'selection' of the insolvency jurisdiction affects the amount of transaction costs, arising from the opening of insolvency proceedings and participation in them (legal, transportation, translation and other costs).

---

[7] European Convention on Certain International Aspects of Bankruptcy, Istanbul, 5.VI.1990. The Istanbul Convention was drafted by a committee of experts subordinate to the European Committee on Legal Co-operation. It was signed by 8 countries (Luxemburg, Turkey, Italy, Greece, Germany, France, Cyprus and Belgium), but ratified only by Cyprus. The Istanbul Convention never entered into force, as this would have required ratification by at least 3 countries.

[8] The influence of the 1995 Convention on the Model Law is evident from its Guide to Enactment and Interpretation (1997), stating in para 18 that '[t]he Model Law takes into account the results of other international efforts, including the negotiations leading to the European Council (EC) Regulation No. 1346/2000 of 29 May 2000 on insolvency proceedings.'

[9] Virgós and Schmit 1996. The report has been frequently referred to by advocates general in their opinions on particular cases involving interpretation of the EIR.

[10] The personal scope of the EIR Recast excludes certain types of companies. According to Article 1(2) EIR Recast, the Regulation shall not apply to proceedings concerning insurance undertakings and credit institutions. These categories of legal entities fall under special regulation, making the problem of COMI less relevant for them. For example, under Directive 2001/24/EC of the European Parliament and of the Council of 4 April 2001 on the reorganisation and winding-up of credit institutions (CIWUD), the competent insolvency forum shall be the home Member State (Article 9 CIWUD), defined as a Member State in which an institution (i.e. bank) has been granted authorisation. For more on EU banking insolvency, see Moss et al. 2017.

This is why ascertainability of COMI is crucial for creditors, as they need to calculate the risks of investment, including risk premiums charged. The Virgós-Schmit Report convincingly states that insolvency is 'a foreseeable risk'. With few exceptions, no business is immune from insolvency.[11] It is therefore important that the insolvency jurisdiction is based on a place known to the debtor's actual and potential creditors. In case of contractual relations and (less so) in property law, parties may adjust their relations *ex ante* or *ex post*, e.g. by choosing an available remedy and a dispute resolution mechanism. This is generally not the case with insolvency law, which curbs party autonomy to ensure collective debt enforcement and *pari passu* distribution of value among the creditors. However, predictability (and suitability) of the international insolvency jurisdiction is not always guaranteed by the existing regulatory environment.

2.3   COMI: Problems Unravelled

Since the adoption of the EIR, substantial progress has been made in clarifying the concept of COMI and its application. A leading role in this has been played by the Court of Justice of the European Union (CJEU). Four years after the EIR had entered into force, in one of the first cases interpreting COMI, *Eurofood IFSC Ltd.*,[12] the CJEU stressed its autonomous 'supranational' meaning. The CJEU noted that COMI must be identified by 'reference to criteria that are both objective and ascertainable by third parties', hence allowing such parties to calculate the risks of dealing with the debtor. The simple presumption in favour of the jurisdiction of the registered office[13] can be rebutted only if objective and ascertainable factors indicate that COMI is somewhere else. This is the case of a 'letterbox' company not carrying out any business activity in the territory of its registered office. In the 2011 case of *Interedil Srl*,[14] the CJEU further reinforced the registered-office presumption by making it impossible to rebut if the debtor's central administration and registered office are situated in the same country.

---

[11] A situation of 'insolvency-proofness' existed in France as applied to establishments of an industrial and commercial character (EICC, or EPIC in their French acronym), such as La Poste. In French administrative law, EPICs are legal entities governed by public law which have distinct legal personality from the state. The status of EPIC entailed a number of legal consequences, including the inapplicability of insolvency and bankruptcy procedures under ordinary law. As a result, creditors of La Poste always had an implied and unlimited state guarantee that their unpaid claims would not be cancelled. This immunity from insolvency was, however, considered to be a source of (unlawful) state aid within the meaning of Article 87(1) EC. See *French Republic v. European Commission*, Case C-559/12 P, ECLI:EU:C:2014:217, Apr. 3, 2014.

[12] *Eurofood IFSC Ltd.*, Case C-341/04, ECLI:EU:C:2006:281, May 2, 2006.

[13] This presumption can be found in Article 3(1) EIR Recast, which states that '[i]n the case of a company or legal person, the place of the registered office shall be presumed to be the centre of its main interests in the absence of proof to the contrary.' The same presumption appeared in Article 3(1) EIR.

[14] *Interedil Srl v. Fallimento Interedil Srl*, Case C-396/09, ECLI:EU:C:2011:671, Oct. 20, 2011.

Despite efforts to achieve predictability, it has proven to be a challenging task. In the words of McCormack, 'the concept of 'centre of main interests' is inherently problematic and certainly capable of varying judicial interpretations.'[15] One of the recent examples supporting this statement is the jurisdictional 'ping-pong' in the insolvency of NIKI, a subsidiary of Air Berlin registered in Austria. At first instance, the District Court of Charlottenburg in Germany accepted that since NIKI's business was operationally controlled and integrated with Air Berlin (Germany), which had practically been NIKI's only customer and sales generator, its COMI was in Germany.[16] The appellate court in Berlin disagreed, finding NIKI's COMI to be in Austria.[17] It noted that in deciding to rebut the registered-office presumption, high demands must be made in order to ensure legal certainty. Shortly after, the Austrian regional court of Korneuburg opened main insolvency proceedings in Austria.

Indeterminacy of COMI can equally play against the interests of a debtor and its management. EU Member States apply divergent rules and approaches when it comes to directors' duties in the period preceding insolvency, sometimes referred to as the 'twilight zone'.[18] Some jurisdictions (e.g. Germany[19]) mandate a strict obligation to file for the opening of insolvency proceedings within a prescribed period of time, imposing severe penalties for failure to do so. Others (e.g. the UK[20]) do not stipulate filing obligations, but regulate directors' behaviour through more flexible wrongful trading rules. In other words, the rules of the game differ from one jurisdiction to another. This is why it is of utmost importance for directors to know which rules apply at any given moment in time. Considering the vagueness of COMI, directors' duties in the period approaching insolvency may become uncertain.[21] This uncertainty together with personal liability of directors is capable of discouraging professional and responsible managers from directing and rescuing failing businesses.

---

[15] McCormack 2009, p. 185. See also Eidenmüller 2005, p. 430, noting that COMI as a standard is 'fuzzy and manipulative, allowing forum shopping in the immediate vicinity of bankruptcy.'

[16] AG Berlin-Charlottenburg, 36n IN 6433/17, Dec. 13, 2017.

[17] LG Berlin, 84 T 2/18, Jan. 8, 2018.

[18] Keay 2015, pp. 140–164. See also INSOL International 2017.

[19] Section 15a German Insolvency Code.

[20] Section 214 Insolvency Act 1986.

[21] For example, in *Simona Kornhaas v. Thomas Dithmar* the CJEU held that liability for the failure to perform the obligation to file for the opening of insolvency proceedings was to be determined according to the German law (*lex concursus*), despite the fact that the debtor company was registered in the UK. This case shows that the applicable company and insolvency rules may fall under different legal (and jurisdictional) regimes, further complicating the position of the debtor's management. See *Simona Kornhaas v. Thomas Dithmar*, C-594/14, ECLI:EU: C:2015:806, Dec. 10, 2015.

On 20 June 2019 the Directive on Preventive Restructuring Frameworks (Restructuring Directive)[22] was adopted. Its main goal is to ensure access to national preventive restructuring frameworks which enable enterprises and entrepreneurs in financial difficulties to continue operating and effectively (financially and operationally) restructure. Among other things, the Restructuring Directive acknowledges that to 'further promote preventive restructurings, it is important to ensure that directors are not dissuaded from exercising reasonable business judgment or taking reasonable commercial risks.'[23] In a situation of jurisdictional uncertainty, this becomes an uphill battle. The next sections discuss three situations or developments, which might highlight the need to revisit the applicable European rules on determining international insolvency jurisdiction.

2.3.1 Uncertainty and European Capital Markets

The lack of clarity with regards to the insolvency jurisdiction and the applicable law deprives creditors of the opportunity to calculate insolvency-related risks, should their counterparty go insolvent. A good case exemplifying this comes from the European capital markets.

As more traditional sources of finance became scarce in the post-financial crisis era, debt capital market products have gained momentum.[24] As a result, many authors highlight the shift in debt structures of companies and corporate groups and the increasingly important role of bondholders in the insolvency (restructuring) process.[25] To ensure investor protection and market efficiency, various regulatory instruments have been adopted in Europe to spur capital flows and cross-border investment. One of the early examples of such regulation is the EC Prospectus Directive.[26] This Directive sought to improve the quality of information provided to

---

[22] Directive (EU) 2019/1023 of the European Parliament and of the Council of 20 June 2019 on preventive restructuring frameworks, on discharge of debt and disqualifications, and on measures to increase the efficiency of procedures concerning restructuring, insolvency and discharge of debt. Unlike the EIR Recast, which creates a binding uniform cross-borderprivate international law framework, the Directive aims at harmonising domestic insolvency (restructuring)laws and needs to be transposed into national laws of Member States.

[23] Recital 70 of the Restructuring Directive. The importance of fostering reasonable risk taking and encouraging business reorganisation is also stressed in Principle B2 of the World Bank's Principles for Effective Insolvency and Creditor/debtor Regimes, 2016.

[24] Finch and Milman 2017, p. 246.

[25] Dakin et al. 2012, p. 120.

[26] Directive 2003/71/EC of the European Parliament and of the Council of 4 November 2003 on the prospectus to be published when securities are offered to the public or admitted to trading and amending Directive 2001/34/EC. The Directive 2003/71/EC is repealed with effect from 21 July 2019 by the Regulation (EU) 2017/1129 of the European Parliament and of the Council of 14 June 2017 on the prospectus to be published when securities are offered to the public or admitted to trading on a regulated market, and repealing Directive 2003/71/EC, COM (2016) 723 Final.

investors by companies wanting to attract external investors in order to raise capital in the European market. The EC Prospectus Directive, with limited exceptions, requires the publication of a prospectus prior to the offering of securities within the European Economic Area (EEA) (Article 3). According to Article 5 of the Prospectus Directive, 'the prospectus shall contain all information which [...] is necessary to enable investors to make an informed assessment of the assets and liabilities, financial position, profit and losses, and prospects of the issuer and of any guarantor, and of the rights attaching to such securities.' Adequate and timely disclosure of information shall protect investors' expectations and help them calculate risks and profits attached to the investment.[27]

Since disclosure represents forward-looking information, on the basis of which investors assess their future earnings, and because insolvency is a calculable risk, it can be expected that prospectuses will cover the insolvency scenarios. Against this background, a selection of prospectuses filed with authorities of the EU Member States has been analysed to find out if this is indeed the case. The chosen prospectuses date from 2009 until 2017 and are therefore covered by the temporal scope of the Prospectus Directive. While this selection does not claim to be comprehensive or in any way representative, it can serve as a starting point in discussing the legitimate expectations of bondholders (investors) in case of the issuers' insolvency. The issuers, whose prospectuses have been studied, include PETRONAS Capital Limited,[28] 4finance S.A.,[29] TUI AG,[30] Photon Energy N.V.[31]

Apart from the usual complexity and extensive length of prospectuses, the first observation to be made is that most of the bond prospectuses mention the issuer's (and guarantor's) insolvency as a potential risk for investors. However, the depth of clarification of such a risk, the explanation of rights of creditors (including their ranking), the applicable law and potential insolvency forum differ significantly. For example, the prospectus of PETRONAS Capital Limited mentions the word 'insolvency/bankruptcy' only once. In contrast, 4finance S.A. allocates a large section describing the insolvency-related risk factors, including enforceability of the notes and guarantees in each of the jurisdictions in which the issuer and the guarantors are organised or incorporated. The difficulty of enforcing guarantees across multiple jurisdictions, caused by ambiguity and unpredictability of applicable insolvency rules has been also stressed in the prospectus of TUI AG. This may be attributed to the problems of determining COMI of the issuer and other parties

---

[27] See Georgakopoulos, arguing that disclosure rules lead to reductions in transaction costs, higher security prices and lower cost of capital. In turn, '[a]ccurate prices make trading less risky and, hence, more appealing.' Georgakopoulos 2017, p. 75.

[28] PETRONAS Capital Limited prospectus dated 12 August 2009, International Securities Identification Number (ISIN) USY68856AH99, Common Code 044509822.

[29] 4finance S.A. prospectus dated 5 August 2016, ISIN XS1417876163, German Securities Identification Number (Wertpapierkennnummer WKN) A181ZP, Common Code 141787616.

[30] TUI AG prospectus dated 21 October 2016, ISIN XS1504103984, Common Code 150410398, WKN A2BPFK.

[31] Photon Energy N.V. prospectus dated 21 September 2017, ISIN DE000A19MFH4.

involved. As explained in the 4finance S.A.'s prospectus, '[t]he determination of where any such company has its "center of main interests" is a question of fact on which the courts of the different EU Member States may have differing and even conflicting views'.[32] The prospectus of Photon Energy N.V. in similar vein states that '[i]n case the Issuer faces financial difficulties, it is not possible to state with certainty, which legal regulations would govern potential opening of insolvency or similar proceedings, or even anticipate the result thereof'.[33]

Even with this limited selection of prospectuses, it becomes clear that insolvency is treated as an inherently unpredictable situation, a kind of a black box, both in terms of the appropriate (or probable) insolvency forum, the validity and enforceability of guarantees, ranking of bondholders' claims and applicable *lex concursus*. This situation is unsatisfactory and goes against the very purpose and principles of securities (i.e. prospectus) and insolvency regulation.

Another layer of complexity arises from the fact that issuers do not usually act on a standalone basis, but instead attract finance as a corporate group, consisting of several legal entities, acting as guarantors or co-issuers. Considering this, the Commission Regulation (EC) No. 809/2004,[34] mentions that prospectuses should disclose the terms, conditions and scope of the guarantee (Annex VI). Thus, if a parent company guarantees performance of debt obligations assumed by its subsidiary, both the description of the guarantee and the guarantor must be given. Minimum disclosure requirements also include organisational structure. If the issuer is part of a corporate group, a brief description of the group and of the issuer's position within it shall be provided. More so, if the issuer is dependent upon other entities within the group, this must be clearly stated together with an explanation of this dependence (Annex IX).

The prospectuses referred to in this chapter describe in detail the position of issuers in corporate group structures. For instance, PETRONAS Capital Limited (Malaysia) is described as a 'wholly-owned special purpose finance subsidiary of PETRONAS, which has been established for the purpose of issuing debt securities and other obligations from time to time to finance the operations of PETRONAS'.[35] This is a typical example of a special purpose company that serves as a financing vehicle for its global parent. 4finance S.A. (Luxembourg) is a part of a consolidated group of companies under the holding company 4finance Holding S.A. 4finance S.A. provides financing to the group companies and is financed through its share capital, external debt and cash from the activities of the group's operating companies.[36] The notes issued by 4finance S.A. are unconditionally and irrevocably

---

[32] Supra note 29, at 244.
[33] Supra note 31, at 50.
[34] Commission Regulation (EC) No. 809/2004 of 29 April 2004 implementing Directive 2003/71/EC of the European Parliament and of the Council as regards information contained in prospectuses as well as the format, incorporation by reference and publication of such prospectuses and dissemination of advertisements. This Regulation contains over two hundred pages of detailed description of information to be disclosed to investors.
[35] Supra note 28, at title page.
[36] Supra note 29, at 135.

guaranteed on a joint and several basis by its parent company and some other group members. Quite the opposite, Photon Energy N.V. is not a special purpose entity, but a holding company with stakes in more than 50 entities, whose activities lie in selection (investment analysis, project acquisition), financing and implementation (investing in the construction) of various projects.[37]

The relative clarity of a group structure and a role performed by an issuer within that structure are crucial in assessing investment risks and, what is more relevant for this article, insolvency risks. More alarming are provisions referring to the occurrence of insolvency itself, since they highlight uncertainty and unpredictability of the insolvency forum and the applicable insolvency law. This brings up the question, to what extent insolvency law and the concept of COMI, in particular, serve the interests of corporate groups and their stakeholders in a situation of financial crisis? The next section of the chapter purports to deal with this question.

2.3.2 Singular Vision and Multinational Enterprise Groups

The principles of (modified) universalism and procedural efficiency, equal treatment of creditors and maximisation of the estate value have played a leading role in the modernisation of insolvency rules in the 20th century, both at the domestic and regional levels. For the most part, such rules possessed two characteristics. First, they were liquidation-oriented, entailing cessation of the debtor's business in the efficient manner and distribution of proceeds from asset realisation.[38] Second, they had a single-entity (i.e. single debtor) insolvency process in mind, thus lacking provisions related to groups of companies. For instance, neither the Directive on the reorganisation and winding up of credit institutions (CIWUD),[39] nor the original EIR (EIR)[40] provided for coordination of insolvency proceedings opened against members of the same corporate group.[41] Neither did the Model Law. It took more than 30 years to agree on a unified set of basic rules and principles underpinning insolvency regulation within the EU, exemplifying complexity and political sensitivity of the matters concerned. Unsurprisingly, the issue of group insolvencies was left out. The difficulty

---

[37] Supra note 31, at 10.

[38] The scope of the EIR covered only 'collective insolvency proceedings which entail the partial or total divestment of a debtor and the appointment of a liquidator.' (Article 1(1) EIR). In addition, according to Article 3(3) EIR, secondary proceedings had to be winding-up proceedings.

[39] Directive 2001/24/EC of the European Parliament and of the Council of 4 April 2001 on the reorganisation and winding up of credit institutions.

[40] See supra note 9, in para 76 highlighting that the Convention (predecessor of the EIR) 'offers no rule for groups of affiliated companies (parent-subsidiary schemes).'

[41] According to the Bank for International Settlements, the global financial crisis has illustrated the shortcomings of the current bank resolution regime and in particular the 'absence of a process for the coordinated resolution of the legal entities in a financial group or financial conglomerate,' thereby limiting the chances of 'coordinated resolution of such cross-border groups or conglomerates.' Bank for International Settlements 2010, p. 24.

of designing a harmonised private international law regime for insolvency of corporate groups in Europe can also be attributed to the fact that the notion of a 'group of companies' did not have any equivalent in some of the domestic laws of the Member States, let alone a single approach at the European level.

The adoption of the EIR Recast in 2015, the Bank Recovery and Resolution Directive (BRRD)[42] in 2014 and the UNCITRAL Model Law on Enterprise Group Insolvency in 2019 signify a second stage in the development of modern insolvency law. The question remains, whether the concept of COMI, developed in, and belonging to, the first stage of insolvency regulation (second half of the 20th century) serves well in the new stage.

There is no universal definition of a corporate group. For instance, the EIR Recast defines 'group of companies' as a parent undertaking and all its subsidiary undertakings (Article 2(13)). The Model Law on Enterprise Group Insolvency (Model Law on Group Insolvency), prepared by the UNCITRAL's Working Group V, characterises an 'enterprise group' as 'two or more enterprises that are interconnected by control or significant ownership'.[43] Mevorach has developed a comprehensive typology of multinational enterprise groups, depending on their level of organisational integration and interdependence.[44] While some groups may consist of relatively self-sufficient business units (e.g. conglomerate group of companies, responsible for separate product/industry lines), others are notable for running a cohesive enterprise. It is the latter type of integrated corporate groups that deserves special attention in insolvency, since the failure of one group member can be contagious and lead to a domino effect for all other group members. The absence of a group-wide solution to financial distress may result in a piecemeal liquidation of assets and suboptimal returns to group creditors.

In a group scenario, problems associated with parallel insolvency proceedings multiply. Protection of enterprise integrity in a single entity, conducting cross-border operations is significantly stronger compared to protection available to cross-border enterprise groups. For example, according Article 20 of the Model Law, recognition of a foreign main proceeding leads to a stay of execution against the debtor's assets. The same effect is created by Article 20 EIR Recast, which extends the effects of the opening of insolvency proceedings under *lex concursus* (typically including enforcement moratorium) to all other EU Member States (except Denmark). Similar

---

[42] Directive 2014/59/EU of the European Parliament and of the Council of 15 May 2014 establishing a framework for the recovery and resolution of credit institutions and investment firms and amending Council Directive 82/891/EEC, and Directives 2001/24/EC, 2002/47/EC, 2004/25/EC, 2005/56/EC, 2007/36/EC, 2011/35/EU, 2012/30/EU and 2013/36/EU, and Regulations (EU) No 1093/2010 and (EU) No 648/2012, of the European Parliament and of the Council.

[43] Article 2(b) Model Law on Group Insolvency.

[44] The classification of prototypes of corporate groups is built around three dimensions, namely insolvency scenario (group collapse v. insolvency of a single member), level of integration and interdependence of corporate group members (from weak (or no) integration to asset integration), degree of management centralisation (from centralised 'head' office to hierarchical networks). For description of prototypes, see Mevorach 2009, pp. 136–147.

tools are unavailable for corporate groups—a stay on individual enforcement actions adopted with regard to one legal entity will usually not apply to another group member, even more so when the latter is located in a different Member State. This situation is further exacerbated by the practice of cross-guarantees, a pervasive arrangement between two or more related companies to provide reciprocal guarantees for each other's liabilities.[45] Cross-guarantees transmit credit risks across parent-subsidiary boundaries, allowing simultaneous filing of claims against several related companies. As a result, the infamous run to court transforms into multiple runs to multiple courts. While cross-guarantees arguably lower the interest rates for the group when it is solvent, they may simultaneously dilute the returns to non-guaranteed creditors upon insolvency.[46] Thus, the collective action and the common pool problems, characteristic of a crisis environment, remain unresolved, generating a ripple effect of failures and potentially upsetting the equality of creditors.

Financial interdependence of corporate groups is neglected by legal separation in insolvency, which can be exploited by some of the creditors. The holdout problem created by the tragedy of 'anticommons'[47] is exacerbated at a group level. When negotiating a restructuring solution for a group as a whole, creditors of some of its members may adopt rent-seeking behaviour, refusing to vote in favour of a plan, even when such a plan is Pareto efficient for all group creditors.[48] Creditors, whose claims are secured by cross-guarantees or numerous pledges, might have even fewer incentives to cooperate and adhere to a restructuring plan if the plan entails deferral of payments or partial debt cancellation.[49] If some of the entities within a

---

[45] Levitin 2019, p. 168.

[46] Squire 2011, p. 608.

[47] In short, anticommons 'present themselves in a situation in which there are several owners or entitled parties, and each of the parties has it within its power to block the use by others.' De Weijs 2012, p. 67. As a result, a single party may sabotage a collectively beneficial solution. Unlike the common pool problem, characterised by overuse of common pool resources (insolvency estate), the problem of anticommons leads to underuse, since each party may veto the use by others. For the discussion of the tragedy of anticommons in the context of restructuring law, see Madaus 2018, pp. 615–647.

[48] An outcome may be considered Pareto efficient (Pareto optimal) where it is not possible to change the situation to make somebody better off without making someone else worse off. In insolvency, the concept of Pareto efficiency may be manifest 'where an insolvency decision or choice produces a greater return to some creditors without reducing the return to any other creditor.' Morrison and Anderson 2013, p. 196.

[49] The hold out position of secured creditors is exacerbated by the existing substantive rules, such as the absolute priority rule (see Section 1129(b)(2) of the U.S. Bankruptcy Code, also suggested in Article 11(2) Restructuring Directive. This rule ensures that a dissenting class of creditors is paid in full before a more junior class can receive any distribution or keep any interest under the restructuring plan. In a group context, the rigidity of the absolute priority rule increases due to the differences in priority of creditors across jurisdictions. For criticism of the rule, see Baird 2016, pp. 785–829; Stanghellini et al. 2018, p. 46, suggesting introduction of a relative priority rule.

group of companies approve the restructuring plan, while others reject it, the utility of the plan and its success become doubtful. Creditors of the rejecting group member will not be bound by the restructuring plan and could pursue enforcement (e.g. foreclosure of the pledged property). Unlike with single entity insolvencies, rules on cram down do not apply in a cross-group framework—there is no cross-entity cram down. As a consequence, the group asset pool is diluted, enterprise value is diminished and restructuring fails.

As noted above, the EIR did not tackle the problem of group insolvencies. Clearly, this instrument was drafted with a single-entity debtor in mind. This singular vision has been supported by the CJEU's decision in *Eurofood IFSC Ltd.*, in which it was stressed that in a situation of a group of companies, COMIs of its members shall be determined separately (entity-by-entity approach). The court relied on the principle of effectiveness, but considered such effectiveness in a narrow sense (single-entity-effectiveness), not paying enough attention to context of a complex multinational enterprise, experiencing financial difficulties in multiple jurisdictions at the same time and trying to pursue restructuring in a single point of entry.[50] The approach taken by the CJEU could be partially explained by the liquidation-oriented nature of the EIR. However, even if the company is destined to be liquidated, the highest possible realisation of its value may depend on whether coordinated group-wide solution (e.g. going concern sale) is available.

As opposed to the EIR, the EIR Recast contains a whole chapter (Chap. 5) dedicated to group insolvencies, with over twenty articles. Nevertheless, the entity-by-entity approach developed by the CJEU, deeply ingrained in the European insolvency law, has not changed with the adoption of the EIR Recast. The latter does not introduce the concept of 'group/enterprise COMI'.[51] Neither does it sanction substantive (pooling of assets and liabilities) or procedural (single insolvency proceeding) consolidation of insolvency proceedings opened against members of a group of companies.[52] It does, however, provide (albeit in the recital) that the court should have the power to open insolvency proceedings for several companies belonging to the same group in a single jurisdiction if the court finds that the

---

[50] The CJEU's failure to address the treatment of related entities in a corporate group with systemic insolvency problems was highlighted by Bufford in Bufford 2007, p. 403.

[51] On the idea of 'enterprise center of main interests (ECOMI)', see Bufford 2012, pp. 685–747.

[52] It should be noted that some European jurisdictions allow for the pooling of assets and liabilities of some or all members of a corporate group, so that a creditor of one member becomes, in essence, a creditor of all members. For instance, art L. 621-2 of the French Commercial Code provides for a consolidation of insolvency proceedings against companies whose property is intermixed or where the corporate body is a sham. However, due to entity shielding and legal separability, substantive consolidation remains extremely rare in Europe. In Case C-191/10, *Rastelli Davide e C. Snc v. Jean-Charles Hidoux*, Case C-191/10, ECLI:EU:C:2011:838 (Dec. 15, 2011), the CJEU had to decide whether the court, having opened the main insolvency proceedings in one Member State (France), could join to those proceedings a second company whose registered office was in another Member State (Italy) solely on the basis that the property of the two companies had been intermixed. The court noted that the legal personality of the two debtors should be respected and that each debtor constituting a distinct legal entity was subject to its own court jurisdiction.

centre of main interests of those companies is located in a single Member State (see Recital 53). Bringing members of a corporate group into a single insolvency forum can significantly reduce transaction costs arising from multiple insolvency proceedings and enhance the chances for a successful restructuring (rescue) of a group as a whole. However, in practice this can be problematic, bearing in mind the singular nature of COMI determination under the EIR Recast. In groups with several operating subsidiaries located in different Member States, locating COMI of all or the majority of group members in the same jurisdiction is highly unlikely. The result is the multiplication of insolvency proceedings, protracted litigation, increased costs, coordination difficulties and reduced chances of a successful group-level resolution.[53]

The rise of corporate groups is not the only development that sits uneasily with current insolvency rules related to insolvency jurisdiction. The next section explores how the modern trends towards decentralisation of business ownership and control challenge our understanding of the centre of main interests.

2.3.3 COMI, New Business Models and Changing Corporate Landscape

Large vertically integrated firms prevailed over the course of the 20th century, the time when the foundation of the modern insolvency law was laid. Throughout that century 'centralisation was the dominant philosophy, a shift brought about largely by the invention of Alexander Graham Bell.'[54] COMI is also a product of that period in history and was therefore affected by the economic and business conditions existing at that time. It should be relatively easy to find the centre of main interests of a railroad company or a vertically integrated manufacturing company. However, the concept becomes less straightforward or practicable in light of the changing corporate landscape. Among relevant developments, proliferation of cooperative (contract-based) enterprises, platform (sharing) economy, and the diminishing role of integrated corporate structures.[55] One can only imagine how the ensuing complexity will affect the 'traditional' approach to corporate structures as well as to finding COMI in a situation of distributed management, where it is either highly problematic or outright impossible to locate the place where the debtor 'conducts the

---

[53] A recent example of a complex group restructuring is the case of the Oi Group, Brazil's largest fixed-line telecoms operator. The restructuring process took around two years, led to extensive litigation in Brazil, the Netherlands and New York and extended to seven legal entities, including two special purpose entities registered in the Netherlands. A large portion of litigation related to the determination of COMIs of Oi's Dutch subsidiaries. For more on the Oi case, see Kokorin and Wessels 2018.

[54] Decentralisation—Idea, The Economist, 2009, https://www.economist.com/news/2009/10/05/decentralisation. Accessed 1 June 2019.

[55] Gilson et al. 2009, pp. 431–502.

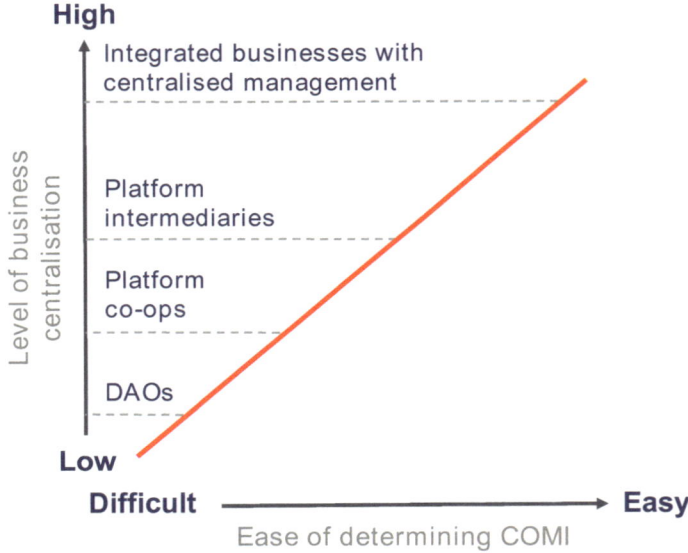

Fig. 2.1 COMI determination and business (management) centralisation

administration of its interests on a regular basis and which is ascertainable by third parties.' The above figure shows a correlation between, on the one hand, the level of business centralisation (from low centralisation to high centralisation of management functions) and the relative ease of determining COMI (from 'difficult' to 'easy'), on the other hand. Thus, highly decentralised business models (like DAOs and unincorporated platform cooperatives (co-ops), addressed below) present the biggest challenge to the concept of COMI and its application in practice (Fig. 2.1).

2.3.3.1   Platform Enterprises and Decentralised Ownership

Ironically, whereas the technological progress of the 19th century (e.g. invention of telegraph and telephone) promoted integration and centralisation of corporate structures,[56] modern technologies seem to pull to the opposite direction by advancing decentralisation. The ease with which information can be accessed and disseminated nowadays simplifies access to corporate decision-making and corporate ownership, e.g. through equity crowdfunding facilitated by platforms like SeedInvest and Wefunder.

---

[56] Before the 19th century, large businesses were typically decentralised. Such was, for instance, the case with the East India Company, whose multi-divisional nature (separation of powers between the board of directors and relatively independent overseas managers (factors)) was highlighted in a number of studies. See Erikson 2014; Anderson et al. 1983, p. 226.

Another decentralising factor arises from the way platform-based businesses operate in general. A good example is Uber, a ride-hailing service, which connects drivers (or driver-partners, as Uber prefers to call them) and riders through a smartphone application. Despite local presence, the largest portion of legal relations with the service-provider is shaped electronically, by downloading and using the application for drivers or riders. Uber portrays itself as a market intermediary and not as a provider of transportation and logistics services.[57] This has an effect on its assets side, as Uber does not own cars.[58] The changing capital structure does not necessarily fit the procedures and even principles of insolvency laws, drafted against the background of assets-heavy industries.[59] Baird persuasively claims that '[f]ew businesses today center around specialised long-lived assets. In a service-oriented economy, the assets walk out the door at 5:00 pm.'[60] Here I make a point that such assets-light platform-based businesses also cast doubt on the rules determining insolvency jurisdiction, particularly when it comes to ascertainability and predictability. Platforms insulate service providers from their users-creditors/debtors by virtue of online space.

According to Uber's Terms of Use, when ordering a Uber-taxi in Spain, Austria or Poland, riders actually enter into a contract with Uber B.V., a private limited liability company established in the Netherlands. While Uber claims that the arranged transportation is then performed by independent third parties, the platform operator remotely controls contracts concluded via the platform with the use of algorithmic rules. Such rules determine, inter alia, a suggested route for each trip and service fees charged.[61] This enables 'platform operators to install data-driven governance structures and exercise control over production and distribution of goods and services without the need for the organisational structure and corporate form of a firm.'[62] Taking into account this algorithmic governance (regulation by technology), it becomes doubtful whether the jurisdiction of the registered office (i.e. the Netherlands) or any other jurisdiction is sufficiently ascertainable either from the drivers' or riders' perspective. Customer and contractor relations are established via the platform's interface, with little knowledge of (or the possibility to know) where Uber actually administers its interests on a regular basis.

Whereas the example of Uber is linked to the issue of notifying creditors about the identity and location of their counterparty (and of its COMI), other examples

---

[57] See Uber's U.S. Terms of Use, effective 13 December 2017.

[58] It does, however, impose requirements on the model, year and capacity of cars used by Uber drivers.

[59] See Roe 2017, p. 215, suggesting that while collective bankruptcy proceedings are needed for industries comprised of big, vertically integrated firms, they may lose appeal in case of decentralised organisational structures.

[60] Baird 2004, p. 82.

[61] These rules are supplemented by the layer of self-regulation, evidenced in the Community Guidelines. https://www.uber.com/en-GH/drive/resources/community-guidelines/. Accessed 1 June 2019. For more on regulatory aspects of platform economy, see Finck 2017.

[62] Busch 2018, forthcoming in: Cantero Gamito and Micklitz 2019.

revolve around dispersed ownership, which is associated with the proliferation of various crowdfunding platforms.[63] As a new form of technology-enabled financial service, 'crowdfunding carries the potential to help better match investors with business projects in need of funding.'[64] Importantly, unlike debt investors (e.g. bond purchasers), equity investors become owners of stock. This is why their position in the insolvency context is very different from that of unsecured creditors. As a matter of practice, in insolvency (restructuring) proceedings equity is either substantially diluted or wiped out completely. Nevertheless, many problems concerning ascertainability, investor protection and risk calculation connected to investment in corporate bonds are just as relevant for equity investment. Dispersed shareholding and control rights, as well as involvement of a crowdfunding platform may conceal the actual decision-making process[65] and make ascertainment of COMI by creditors more problematic.

2.3.3.2 Blockchain and Decentralised Management

But an even larger challenge lies in technological developments, characterised by a distributed nature, trustless consensus mechanics and undisputed reliability.[66] The first and by far the most famous example of the latest inventions is Bitcoin, a cryptocurrency that operates on a P2P basis, i.e. without an intermediary or central authority such as governments or banks. All transactions between Bitcoin users are verified and validated by other users and recorded in a public distributed ledger ('blockchain'). Despite the fact that the cryptocurrency did not become prominent in retail transactions, Bitcoin has turned into an investment asset, and (maybe more importantly) introduced the blockchain technology into the world. Blockchain makes it possible to record multiple transactions in a decentralised and distributed manner so that such transactions cannot be altered retroactively.

Apart from its use for cryptocurrencies, blockchain allowed the creation of the so-called DAOs or decentralised autonomous organisations, which in essence are computer codes that allow people from all over the world with access to the Internet to anonymously (pseudonymously, to be more accurate) enter into series of transactions, which are enforced and recorded on blockchain. They are therefore globally decentralised (not linked to any particular jurisdiction) and distributed among their users.[67] Without going too far in explaining the technical side of DAOs, it is sufficient to say that they allow a partnership-like 'entity' to exist,

---

[63] Schwartz 2015, p. 634.

[64] EC Proposal for a Regulation of the European Parliament and of the Council on European Crowdfunding Service Providers (ECSP) for Business, COM (2018) 113 final, 2018.

[65] See Walthoff-Borm et al. 2018, noting on p. 317 that 'the more ownership becomes dispersed, the more challenging it will be to align the interests of all crowd investors.'

[66] This part draws on Kokorin 2017.

[67] De Filippi and Wright 2018, p. 148.

attract new investor-users and make decisions by majority voting of its users. As a result, the separation of ownership and control becomes less prominent. In turn, access to (corporate) governance becomes more open. This makes DAOs more similar to the Athenian polis (ancient Greek city-state) with its (direct) democracy than a corporation with separate ownership and control as famously described by Berle and Means.[68]

A DAO is based on a decentralised model—its members may be unaware of who other members are and which countries they come from. Besides, there is no central authority or management, as decisions are made by DAO's members (so called 'token holders') themselves by way of voting on proposals. Each transaction is kept on the blockchain. Given these characteristics, it becomes especially problematic (if not impossible) to connect a DAO to any particular jurisdiction. One of the first DAOs was The DAO. The DAO acted as a venture capital vehicle, whose members acquired 'ownership' stakes by spending cryptocurrency called Ether (digital value token of the Ethereum blockchain) on The DAO's 'shares' or tokens. The DAO had no physical address, employees or formal management. Even though the exact legal status of The DAO (or any DAO for that matter), is unclear, whereas risks (both regulatory and operational) remain high, it managed to raise more than USD 150 million during a feverish, 27-day token sale. Yet a then unforeseen flaw in The DAO's code was exploited, resulting in a USD 60 million loss and the collapse of the project.[69]

Despite the fact that The DAO's fate was doomed, its failure did not undermine the prospects for decentralised organisations.[70] Modern technological advancements, allowing 'trustless' decision-making between anonymous persons will play an ever-bigger role in the future. And with this rise of decentralisation in mind, it will be increasingly difficult to find a linking factor to any single jurisdiction. The conservative criteria formulated for locating COMI, especially the idea that it

---

[68] Berle and Means 1932.

[69] For more on the DAO and its collapse, see D Siegel, Understanding the DAO Attack, Coindesk, 25 June 2016. https://www.coindesk.com/understanding-dao-hack-journalists. Accessed 1 June 2019.

[70] The creation of self-organising companies that run via software and allow people to collaborate with each other without command-and-control type of internal regulation or formal incorporation is foreseen by a number of innovative startups. For instance, The Colony Protocol proposes the creation of a 'new "Nature of the Firm" by significantly reducing both the transaction costs of the market exchange mechanism for labour, and trust required for people to work together.' This should result from integration of decentralised and self-regulating division of labour, decision making, and financial management into the applications. See Colony. Technical White Paper, 27 July 2018. https://colony.io/whitepaper.pdf. Accessed 1 June 2019. On the discussion of Colony's proposed capital and governance structure, see also Mannan 2019. Another example is Aragon Network, which aims at providing a 'mechanism for pseudo-anonymous blockchain entities, including decentralised autonomous organizations (DAOs) and individuals, to create flexible human-readable agreements that are enforceable on-chain.' See Aragon Network White Paper. https://github.com/aragon/whitepaper. Accessed 1 June 2019.

should be ascertainable by third parties, simply does not fit the new decentralised world paradigm. In decentralised entities, where there is no formal management, decision-making is inherently democratic. There are no physical assets—only digital tokens and claims arising from them. Besides, such entities do not have offices or officers, while the stakeholders might be scattered around the globe.

Algorithmic governance, embraced by new platform-based business models, and decentralised decision-making, facilitated by blockchain technology provide reasons to doubt whether linking insolvency jurisdiction to the place of 'administration of interests on a regular basis' or the registered office remains operational and feasible. The next section considers several ways that can make insolvency jurisdiction rules more up-to-date with modern technological, corporate and financial developments.

2.4 The 'New Age' and New Approaches to Insolvency Jurisdiction

In the previous sections, we introduced the concept of COMI as currently applied under the EIR Recast. It was shown that there are difficulties of using COMI as a jurisdictional link to determine the insolvency forum. The lack of clarity and ascertainability of COMI-jurisdiction appears unsettling and leads to a situation in which insolvency is treated as an unpredictable event, both in terms of the insolvency forum and related applicable law. As a result, up to the point of a default (or even after the default), investors struggle in calculating insolvency-related risks of their investment and, similarly, other creditors face the same struggle. The EIR Recast attempts to tackle the endemic concern over COMI's vagueness with the introduction of a presumption that a company's registered office coincides with its COMI (Article 3(1) EIR Recast). This is a half-hearted solution. Firstly, the value assigned to the registered office presumption and the comparable ease of its rebuttal vary depending on the interpretation given by a particular court or a judge, as exemplified by NIKI's insolvency, discussed above. Secondly, the presumption falls short of addressing situations of groups of companies as the legal separation (insulation), facilitated by the presumption, may ignore economic reality and frustrate group-wide restructuring. Thirdly, company registration plays a lesser role, or is less ascertainable, in the context of decentralised ownership and decision-making. For example, decentralised autonomous organisations or platform cooperatives may exist without formal corporate registration and operate through algorithms (smart contacts).

This section of the chapter looks at three 'enhanced' approaches to the treatment of insolvency jurisdiction. These approaches are not meant to substitute or undermine the prevailing doctrine of COMI, embraced both by the Model Law and the EIR Recast (although, not necessarily in a consistent way), thus cumulatively covering around 60 jurisdictions.[71] Instead, they serve the purpose of supplementing the application of the COMI concept.

The chapter began by stressing that the power of creditors and other stakeholders to make a choice of the insolvency forum is significantly curtailed. The starting point is that parties cannot freely select the forum where the resolution of the debtor's insolvency should take place. This limitation to party autonomy can be attributed to the never really discussed pre-occupation that 'insolvency law' is 'public law' and should therefore be handled by courts, which are public institutions. Another attribution is formed by the fears of abusive forum shopping, where COMI is shifted for the purposes of benefiting certain actors (e.g. debtor's management and owners) to the detriment of the general body of creditors.[72] While the dangers of abusive forum shopping must not be underestimated, the real negative economic effects of such practice is difficult to calculate. Besides, value-destructive forum shopping may be addressed by less intrusive and more narrowly tailored means than outright prohibition of insolvency-forum contracting (as it should preferably be referred to).[73] In light of this, it may be suggested that serious consideration needs to be given to the possibilities of parties (debtors and creditors) to shape *ex ante* and *ex post* the insolvency process, including the international insolvency jurisdiction.

The previous section highlighted that insolvency stakeholders cannot freely choose the insolvency forum and the applicable insolvency law. This limitation has two major consequences. First, creditors cannot adequately calculate investment risks *ex ante*, since insolvency remains outside the scope of their control. Second, upon insolvency, *ex post* control over the choice of the insolvency jurisdiction and *lex concursus* is further restricted. This leads to suboptimal results, as credit costs are increased, while the option of selecting the optimal insolvency regime (and its tools) to effectively address financial distress becomes unavailable. The outcome ultimately hurts both creditors and debtors.

In the 1980s, the Creditors' Bargain theory was proposed to offer a comprehensive normative theory of insolvency (bankruptcy) law.[74] According to this

---

[71] The term 'centre of main interests' is also used in the Cape Town Convention on International Interests in Mobile Equipment (2001), covering more than 70 states, as well as the European Union. For the status of the Convention, see https://www.unidroit.org/status-2001capetown. Accessed 1 June 2019.

[72] According to Recital 29 EIR Recast, '[t]his Regulation should contain a number of safeguards aimed at preventing fraudulent or abusive forum shopping.' For more on insolvency forum shopping, see Ringe 2017, pp. 38–59; Eidenmüller 2009.

[73] Such measures are already ingrained in the structure of the EIR Recast. For example, Article 3 (1) EIR Recast contains the so called 'suspension periods' for COMI shifts carried out shortly before the debtor files for insolvency. The EIR Recast provides that the change of the debtor's registered office within 3 months prior to the insolvency filing disables the registered office presumption. This is a mandatory and inflexible rule, which cannot be overridden by the parties' consent. Thus, the fact that the COMI-shift has been approved by the debtor and all (or substantial majority) of its creditors, and is beneficial for all the parties concerned, has no legal effect.

[74] Jackson 1982, pp. 857–907; Jackson 1986.

theory, insolvency rules can be seen through the prism of an implicit bargain reached by creditors of a debtor. In other words, insolvency is viewed as a system 'designed to mirror the agreement one would expect the creditors to form among themselves were they able to negotiate such an agreement from an *ex ante* position.'[75] This chapter does not aim at supplying a comprehensive overview of this theory. Neither does it claim that this theory can fully explain or support the observable shift of insolvency law to a contract paradigm. Instead, it suggests that the Creditors' Bargain theory provides a useful explanatory toolbox and can be seen as a starting point to the analysis of current insolvency rules and ways to improve them, extending far beyond the justification of the collective nature of insolvency proceedings.[76] From the creditors' point of view, inefficiencies created by the blanket prohibition of the *ex ante* or *ex post* choice of insolvency forum and insolvency law are obvious. These inefficiencies may lead to the increase in strategic costs (e.g. calculating insolvency-related risks or negotiating over additional security), decrease in the aggregate pool of assets (e.g. due to inadequate insolvency regime or costly COMI-shifts) and the rise of administrative inefficiencies (e.g. costs of COMI-related litigation or communication between insolvency practitioners and courts).

In this context, it may serve the collective interests of creditors as a group to agree on the insolvency-related conditions in advance or *ex post*. Such an agreement could result in the reduction of uncertainty, which itself must be viewed as a virtue, leading to improved efficiency of insolvency proceedings. In the absence of certainty, incentives are created for both the debtor and its creditors to manipulate (search for self-serving) insolvency jurisdiction and/or the applicable law. As noted above, uncertainty equally plays against the management of ailing businesses, since the prospects of personal liability act as a deterrent to active management. Consequently, directors may embrace conservative, risk-minimising strategies, shifting from 'an active management mode to one of passive asset-preservation.'[77] These considerations make it likely that a general unsecured creditor and a debtor will agree to the possibility of *ex ante* or *ex post* contracting for the insolvency forum. Such an agreement will arguably lead to the decrease in strategic costs, an increase in the aggregate pool of assets and reduction of administrative inefficiencies.

The Creditors' Bargain theory deals with hypothetical or implicit contracting, which is attributed to practical difficulties of reaching an agreement between widely dispersed and constantly changing creditors. However, decades have passed since the model of creditors' bargain was developed and the various forms of actual contracts shaping the course of insolvency process have appeared in practice. One notable development is the rise and expansion of secured credit in capital structures

---

[75] Ibid., p. 860.

[76] The Creditors' Bargain theory was initially suggested by Thomas Jackson to explain insolvency law's role in resolving a common pool problem. By imposing collective enforcement, insolvency law prevents individual race to court and preserves the integrity of the insolvency estate.

[77] Stilson 1995, p. 91.

of insolvent companies.[78] Secured creditors derive their priority and power from contractual arrangements, which guarantee them a preferential position in insolvency and the ability to exercise significant control over the insolvency process. In some jurisdictions (e.g. the Netherlands[79]), secured creditors are essentially immune from insolvency proceedings. In others (e.g. the US), they typically lead insolvency proceedings and dictate the conditions for the business sale.[80] Thus, contractually agreed rights presuppose a certain position in insolvency. Another example of contracts affecting insolvency proceedings are intercreditor agreements or agreements between creditor(s) and a debtor. Such agreements may entail claim subordination, where one creditor or a group of creditors agree to subordinate their rights in insolvency, therefore contracting out of the *pari passu* principle.[81] In the famous case *Re Maxwell Communications Corp. plc (No. 2)*,[82] the English court upheld the effectiveness of contractual subordination, rejecting the argument that it contravened the mandatory (public) rules of insolvency law. More novel forms of insolvency-related contracting include restructuring support agreements, used primarily in the US to lock up the contractual arrangements and support of a particular plan later implemented by way of a pre-packaged deal. Such arrangements provide certainty and ensure 'a clearer, quicker, and more reliable path toward exit from Chapter 11.'[83]

These and other instances of contractual 'regulation' of insolvency allowed Skeel and Triantis to conclude that the US insolvency (bankruptcy) law is considerably less mandatory than it appears to be and that the new contract paradigm seems to emerge (even if in a somewhat inconsistent way).[84] In this shift towards private ordering, contracting during or prior to insolvency as an alternative or next to judicial decision-making refers primarily to substantive effects of insolvency,[85] such as the position of a creditor in the ranking of claims or the power to control the

---

[78] See American Bankruptcy Institute Commission to Study the Reform of Chapter 11, 2012–2014 Final Report and Recommendations; Nocilla 2017, pp. 60–81.

[79] According to Article 57 Dutch Bankruptcy Act, pledgees and mortgagees may exercise their (preferential recovery) rights as if there was no bankruptcy.

[80] It has been noted that without consent from a secured creditor, it may not be possible to sell property in a 363 Sale free and clear of liens. See Simpson and Goffman in Mallon and Waisman 2011, p. 15.

[81] Goode 2011, p. 241; Finch and Milman 2017, p. 530.

[82] *Re Maxwell Communications Corp Plc (No. 2)*, [1994] 1 All E.R. 737.

[83] Baird 2017, p. 604. Chapter 11 of the US Bankruptcy Code (Chapter 11, Title 11, United States Code) generally provides for the reorganisation of debts of financially distressed companies. It may be used to preserve the legal entity or sell its business as a going concern.

[84] Skeel and Triantis 2018.

[85] An increase in the ability of debt holders (sometimes referred to as 'creditors in possession') to influence the conduct of business prior and during the course of the Chapter 11 proceedings has also been noted by Rasmussen, who mentions among the instruments of control, covenants in credit agreements, loan-to-own strategies, appointment of a chief restructuring officer, debtor in possession (DIP) financing, plan support and restructuring support agreements, etc. See Rasmussen 2018.

course of insolvency proceedings, e.g. through the provision of post-petition financing. The question arises whether this encroachment of private law mechanisms to regulate the insolvency process also extends to issues of insolvency jurisdiction. As explained above, the conventional wisdom is that parties cannot contract on this matter.[86] However, in practice and in law various forms of insolvency forum choice have emerged.

2.4.1 Choice of Insolvency Forum in a Contract

Even though the choice of the insolvency jurisdiction in a contract concluded between a creditor and a debtor is not legally enforceable at the current time, making such a choice can still be a good idea. The reason being that the parties' agreement as to the debtor's COMI enters the realm of their expectations and is therefore ascertainable from the moment of contracting. Unless the agreed COMI is clearly contrary to the economic or business (administration of interests) reality, the selection of the insolvency forum should not be easily ignored.

There is no statistics on how widespread the practice of COMI choice is. Hamilton and Hair report that it is rather common in the UK market for lenders to ask for a representation from a borrower that its COMI is located in a certain jurisdiction, and for an undertaking not to move the COMI without the lenders' consent or notification.[87] However, there are very few instances of judicial interpretation of provisions allocating insolvency jurisdiction. In a recent case *In the matter of Videology Limited*,[88] the court had to interpret the following warranty and representation as to the COMI of the debtor: 'For the purposes of the Council of the European Union Regulation No. 1346/2000 on Insolvency Proceedings ("the Regulation") [the debtor's] centre of main interest (as that term is used in Article 3(1) of the Regulation) is situated in England and it has no "establishment" (as that term is used in Article 2(h) of the Regulation) in any other jurisdiction.' Interestingly, the sole director of the debtor argued that this COMI-related clause contained 'boilerplate' representations which were not given 'any particular thought to at the time.' However, the court did not accept the characterisation of this clause as mere 'boilerplate'. In finding otherwise, it noted that a clause expressly referred to the EIR and identified the COMI of the debtor as being in England in the agreement predominantly between US parties and governed by US law. Besides,

---

[86] For early discussion on the possibility of choice of the insolvency forum, see Rasmussen 1992; Rasmussen 1997; Schwartz 1993.

[87] Hamilton and Hair, County Report—Great Britain, in Pannen 2007, p. 651. The possibility of including COMI-related representations and warranties is also supported by the Act borrower's guide to the LMA facilities agreement for leveraged transactions, Association of Corporate Treasurers, October 2008, pp. 106–108.

[88] *In the matter of Videology Limited and In the matter of the Cross-Border Insolvency Regulations* [2018] EWHC 2186 (Ch).

the director acknowledged that the purpose of the inclusion of such a clause was to 'provide certainty to the lenders as to the jurisdiction in which any insolvency proceedings in relation to the [debtor] would take place.'[89] According to the court, the express representations in the financing documents gave strong support of finding the debtor's COMI in the agreed jurisdiction.

The importance of safeguarding parties' expectations in financial contracts is undeniable. However, this does not mean that parties are free in their insolvency-related contracting. For instance, in order to preserve integrity of insolvency proceedings or ensure centralisation of restructuring efforts, it should not be possible for a debtor to choose a different insolvency forum in various contracts with creditors. The unacceptability of allowing the debtor to contract with creditors on an opt-out basis has also been emphasised by the authors of the Creditors' Bargain theory.[90] This is why it is rather surprising that such an opt-out exists in practice and is frequently called the 'Gibbs rule'.[91]

Despite the fact that the law governing a contract is usually not determinative for international insolvency jurisdiction, the chosen law can have a decisive effect on the course and results of debt restructuring. The century-old Gibbs rule, as applied by English courts, effectively means that English law-governed debt cannot be discharged or compromised by a foreign insolvency proceeding, unless the creditor had submitted to such proceeding. Discharge of a debt or its alteration under the insolvency law of a foreign country is only treated as discharge in England if it is done under the law applicable to the contract. Thus, in a recent case of *Bakhshiyeva v. Sberbank of Russia*,[92] the English court refused to grant a moratorium to prevent creditors from commencing enforcement actions against assets of a foreign bank, which was subject to restructuring abroad. As long as a debt instrument is governed by English law, it is immune from the effect of non-English restructurings. The Gibbs rule has been heavily criticised in academic literature as undermining the principles of international insolvency law, such as universality (modified universalism), efficiency of insolvency (restructuring) proceedings and *pari passu*.[93] It also facilitates non-cooperative behaviour and enhances the position of hold-out creditors, potentially undermining value-creating restructuring attempts.

---

[89] Ibid., para 69.

[90] Supra note 74, at 866.

[91] The name of the rule comes from the case of *Antony Gibbs & Sons v La Société Industrielle et Commerciale des Métaux* (1890) LR 25 QBD 399, in which the English Court of Appeal held that 'a debt governed by English law cannot be discharged or compromised by a foreign insolvency proceeding. Indeed, the proposition goes further: discharge of a debt under the insolvency law of a foreign country is only treated as a discharge therefrom in England if it is a discharge under the law applicable to the contract.'

[92] *Bakhshiyeva v. Sberbank of Russia* [2018] EWHC 59 (Ch), upheld on appeal.

[93] See Ramesh, who noted that '[t]he Gibbs principle is a relic of a different legal and economic era that ought to be consigned to the annals of history.' In Ramesh 2017, p. 42. See also Fletcher, who claimed that the 'Gibbs doctrine belongs to an age of Anglocentric reasoning which should be consigned to history.' Fletcher 2005, para 2.129.

Thus, under the Gibbs rule, the choice of law governing the contract indirectly allows parties to select the insolvency forum. In other words, the choice of law becomes the choice of the insolvency jurisdiction. Previously, it was stated that an *ex ante* agreement as to the COMI can be beneficial and lead to a decrease in strategic costs and a reduction of administrative costs. The Gibbs scenario is the example of the opposite, to the extent that it allows selective choice of the insolvency jurisdiction, which disrupts the otherwise centralised resolution of financial distress. The possibility of individual enforcement actions in the absence of a parallel English proceeding (e.g. scheme of arrangement) may subvert the collective nature of insolvency proceedings. In the hypothetical bargain situation, no creditor would agree to be bound to the collective system unless it were a compulsory system binding on all other creditors, including those who might agree on English law as law governing their contractual relations with the debtor.

2.4.2 Synthetic and 'Reverse' Synthetic Insolvency Proceedings

The previous sub-section of this chapter provides an example of contractual regulation of international insolvency jurisdiction. It involves an agreement reached by a debtor and its creditor(s). However, the possibility of contracting or, broadly speaking, constructing the insolvency jurisdiction in cross-border insolvency cases is not limited to agreements in a traditional sense. Thus, in the case of *Collins & Aikman Europe SA*,[94] the High Court of Justice authorised the English-appointed joint administrators of a group of companies to implement the assurances given earlier to creditors in the relevant European jurisdictions and hence to *pro tanto* depart from the application of the ordinary provisions of English law, the law of the main proceedings. The case concerned Collins & Aikman group, which was a leading supplier of automotive components, typically plastic and soft-trim products used in the interiors of motor vehicles. In Europe, the group operated through 24 legal entities spread over ten jurisdictions. In 2005, these entities applied for the UK court to open insolvency proceedings. Subsequently, insolvency proceedings were opened in the UK against all 24 companies, including those registered on the Continent (for example, in Spain, Sweden, Germany, Belgium, Italy and The Netherlands).

The appointed joint administrators immediately recognised that although the European companies were incorporated in several different European countries, they formed a closely-linked group, many of the functions of which were organised on a Europe-wide rather than on a national basis. The strategy developed by the administrators was based on this understanding and included the adoption of a coordinated approach to the continuation of the businesses. Administrators were, however, well

---

[94] *Re Collins & Aikman Europe SA and other companies* [2006] EWHC 1343 (Ch).

aware that, whilst the main proceedings were in England, creditors remained entitled to seek the opening of secondary proceedings in any of the other countries where a relevant company had an 'establishment'. To avoid such secondary proceedings, oral assurances were given by or on behalf of the joint administrators to local creditors that their claims would be dealt with in accordance with the relevant (foreign) insolvency law and the respective ranking of claims. As a result, creditors were to receive the benefits of the secondary proceedings (such as preferential payments), while such proceedings did not formally exist. Thus, the terms 'synthetic' or 'virtual' secondary proceedings were proposed. Ultimately, the English court supported this very practical and commercially-driven solution and empowered the administrators to implement any assurances that they had earlier given.

The concepts of party autonomy and judicial effectiveness underpin the operation of this legal innovation. The following interpretation given by Ramesh should be endorsed:

> [w]hen the English court sanctioned the arrangement, it was in effect endorsing the parties' autonomy to determine the jurisdiction that the insolvency proceedings ought to be carried out in.[95]

As a result of the administrators' actions and the willingness of the courts to support them, the group resolution became more predictable, centralised and cost-efficient.[96]

The acceptance of practical utility of synthetic proceedings has led to the inclusion of Article 36 in the EIR Recast. According to this article, in order to avoid the opening of secondary insolvency proceedings, the insolvency practitioner in the main insolvency proceedings may give a unilateral undertaking ('undertaking') in respect of the assets located in the Member State in which secondary insolvency proceedings could be opened. This undertaking guarantees that when distributing those assets or the proceeds received as a result of their realisation, the main insolvency practitioner will comply with the distribution and priority rights under domestic law that creditors would have if secondary insolvency proceedings were opened in that Member State.[97] If an undertaking complies with Article 36 and adequately protects the general interests of local creditors, the court asked to open secondary proceedings shall refuse to do so (Article 38(2) EIR Recast). Thus, the judicial innovation of *Collins & Aikman Europe SA* has now been institutionalised at the EU level.[98] It pursues two major objectives. Firstly, it allows for the centralisation of control over the major decisions affecting the debtor and the insolvency estate, such as the development of a cohesive restructuring plan, in one

---

[95] Ramesh 2018, p. 6.

[96] Pottow 2011, p. 585.

[97] On the nature of 'undertaking' as an instrument of private and public nature, see Wessels 2014, pp. 63–110.

[98] On the implementation of Article 36 EIR Recast at the domestic level, see Realisation of the EU Insolvency Regulation (EIR 2015) in national (procedural) law of the Member States, CERIL Report 2018-1 on Insolvency Regulation (Recast) and National Procedural Rules, 2018.

jurisdiction. Secondly, it safeguards the rights and legitimate expectations of local and preferential creditors by ensuring compliance with the priority rights guaranteed under the relevant domestic insolvency laws.

It must be noted that an undertaking, as prescribed by Article 36 EIR Recast, is always one-sided and only works in vertical relations, that is, between main insolvency practitioner (main proceedings) and local creditors (secondary proceedings). It cannot be applied to avoid the opening of main insolvency proceedings, e.g. by a request from the insolvency practitioner appointed in territorial proceedings. This is a serious restriction, particularly for insolvencies of groups of companies, which may require concentration of insolvency proceedings at the location of both the COMIs and establishments of group members. Interestingly, the evasion of main insolvency proceedings happened in *Re Videology Ltd.* referred to above. In that case, Videology Ltd. (debtor), the UK registered entity, was part of the joint efforts to sell the business of the whole corporate group as a going concern. For that reason, both the debtor and its parent company filed voluntary bankruptcy petitions under Chapter 11 of the US Bankruptcy Code.[99] The debtor asked the court in the UK to recognise the US proceedings as foreign main proceedings to secure a moratorium on individual enforcement actions and preclude initiation of parallel insolvency proceedings. Having closely studied the facts of the case, the UK court was not persuaded that the debtor's COMI was in the US. It concluded that COMI of Videology Ltd. was in the UK, the jurisdiction of its incorporation.[100] What is more important is the type and effects of relief granted by the court.

The court first noted that there should be very good reasons to restrict or prohibit creditors of a company with its COMI in the UK from seeking to commence main insolvency proceedings there. Nevertheless, this was found to be the case. Allowing the business and assets of the debtor to be sold as part of a coordinated sale pursuant to the Chapter 11 proceeding in the US was beneficial to all creditors of Videology Ltd.[101] In this respect, the opening of parallel (main) insolvency proceedings in the UK would have disturbed this smoothly running process. This cost-benefit analysis (i.e. Pareto efficiency, referred to above) has led to the pragmatic decision, essentially driven by the parties' choices. The court held that it was appropriate to grant the relief, in effect entrusting the realisation and distribution of the entirety of the

---

[99] Chapter 11, Title 11, United States Code.

[100] The EIR/EIR Recast apply only if COMI is within the EU (with the exception of Denmark). Therefore, if the UK court had found that the debtor's COMI was in the US or in another non-EU country, the EIR/EIR Recast would not have been applicable. In such a case, the English court would need to rely on its national conflict of law rules, including the Cross Border Insolvency Regulations 2006 (CBIR), implementing the Model Law. In *Re Videology Ltd.* the English court relied on the CBIR to determine the relief granted to a foreign (non-EU) non-main proceeding. This is because the EIR/EIR Recast do not regulate relations with non-EU countries (i.e. the US). For more on the territorial scope of the EIR Recast and its drawbacks, see Nisi 2017.

[101] According to the court, the anticipated outcome of a coordinated sale of the business of the group in the US would result in the payment of £0.07 per £1. By contrast, 'a stand-alone liquidation or administration of the debtor and collection of its receivables would be expected to achieve a return of only about £0.01 per £1.' See supra note 88, para 88.

assets of the debtor to the US proceeding, the jurisdiction of an establishment, and imposing a court-controlled moratorium on creditors' claims in the UK. Thus, the opening of main insolvency proceedings was avoided (therefore, 'reverse' synthetic proceedings).[102] This is a good example of a more advanced construction of the insolvency jurisdiction in a cross-border insolvency scenario, involving several members of the corporate group.

The described case relied on the Model Law, providing for the possibility of granting flexible discretionary relief under its Article 21. Would reverse synthetic proceedings be available under the EIR Recast? The analysis of the EIR Recast framework leads to the negative answer. First and foremost, Article 36 EIR Recast applies only to an undertaking given by a main insolvency practitioner in respect of assets located in a Member State where secondary proceedings could be opened. The corresponding Article 38(2) mandating the court to refuse the opening of proceedings in case of an undertaking, refers only to secondary proceedings. The refusal of the opening of main proceedings is not mentioned. Another practical limitation stems from the difficulty of opening territorial proceedings in the absence of main insolvency proceedings. For example, Article 3(4) EIR Recast lists a number of rigid conditions under which territorial proceedings are allowed.[103] Besides, on a more fundamental structural level, the nature of territorial and secondary proceedings under the EIR Recast is strictly territorial. This nature does not easily accommodate the geographical extension beyond the territory of such proceedings.[104]

There might be compelling reasons to allow the use of 'reverse' synthetic insolvency proceedings in Europe, particularly in the context of resolution within corporate groups. The centralisation of insolvency proceedings opened against members of a corporate group in a single 'point of entry' is significantly restricted by the notion of COMI, as found in Article 3(1) EIR Recast. The concept of establishment,[105] permitting the initiation of secondary proceedings, could

---

[102] The term 'reverse synthetic proceedings' was coined by Kannan Ramesh in Ramesh 2018. The use of the word 'reverse' should indicate that as opposed to normal synthetic proceedings (prevention of *secondary* proceedings), 'reverse' synthetic proceedings prevent the opening of *main* insolvency proceedings.

[103] The territorial insolvency proceedings may only be opened prior to the opening of main insolvency proceedings where (a) main insolvency proceedings cannot be opened because of the conditions prescribed by *lex concursus*; or (b) the opening of territorial insolvency proceedings is requested by: (i) a creditor whose claim arises from or is in connection with the operation of an establishment situated within the territory of the Member State where the opening of territorial proceedings is requested; or (ii) a public authority which, under the law of the Member State within the territory of which the establishment is situated, has the right to request the opening of insolvency proceedings.

[104] This extension is only permitted in exceptional circumstances, such as where the application for the return of assets or a transaction avoidance claim is filed in a foreign court pursuant to Article 21(2) EIR Recast.

[105] According to Article 2(10) EIR Recast, 'establishment' means any place of operations where a debtor carries out or has carried out in the 3-month period prior to the request to open main insolvency proceedings a non-transitory economic activity with human means and assets.

represent a tool to open territorial (non-main) proceedings with the effect 'as if' such proceedings are actually main insolvency proceedings. This approach has distinct advantages of adaptivity and increased flexibility.

Whereas the prospects of reverse synthetic proceedings in Europe remain unclear, the door for them may be opened with the adoption of a new UNCITRAL Model Law on Group Insolvency, briefly referred to above. The idea to create a new model law, specifically addressing the issue of insolvency of enterprise groups emerged in 2013. Since then the UNCITRAL Working Group V (Insolvency Law) has been working on the draft provisions of the new model law. The Model Law on Group Insolvency in Articles 30 and 31 creates a framework for reverse synthetic proceedings. It empowers an insolvency representative, appointed in non-main proceedings, to give an undertaking to treat creditors as if main proceedings have been opened. In this case, a court in the jurisdiction of the debtor's COMI may stay or decline to commence main proceedings. Arguably, resolution of insolvency in a non-main forum may run afoul of prior expectations of creditors and other third parties. This is why, according to the Guide to enactment of the Model Law on Group Insolvency, 'departing from that basic principle of commencing proceedings on the basis of COMI should be limited to exceptional circumstances, namely to cases where the benefits, in terms of efficiency, largely outweigh any negative effect on creditors' expectations in particular and legal certainty in general.'[106]

The idea of choosing and altering the insolvency forum for the sake of efficient group resolution and well-functioning administration of the insolvency estate is quite remarkable. The instrument of an undertaking, whether given to avoid the opening of main or non-main (secondary) proceedings, creates a binding and enforceable obligation upon the insolvency estate.[107] This can be characterised as an extension of the private law relations arising from a contract (or unilateral promise) to traditionally public-interest driven and protected area of insolvency law,[108] and the issue of international insolvency jurisdiction in that area, in particular.

2.4.3   Selection of a Group Coordination Forum

Alongside the mechanism of synthetic proceedings, the EIR Recast offers another tool, which gives creditors and debtors additional leeway to decide and construct their own fate in insolvency. This tool is called 'group coordination proceedings'. Group coordination proceedings is an innovation of the EIR Recast. It has been

---

[106] Enterprise group insolvency: guide to enactment of the draft model law (as contained in A/CN.9/WG.V/WP.161), 20 September 2018, para 206.

[107] Ibid., para 188.

[108] As famously stated by Sir Peter Millett, '[n]o branch of the law is moulded more by considerations of national economic policy and commercial philosophy,' than insolvency law. Millett 1997, p. 109.

introduced '[w]ith a view to further improving the coordination of the insolvency proceedings of members of a group of companies, and to allow for a coordinated restructuring of the group' (Recital 54 EIR Recast). In essence, group coordination proceedings are separate from any other insolvency proceedings and can be seen as a legal superstructure, imposed on (all or some) insolvency proceedings of corporate group members.

Coordinated treatment of insolvency proceedings in a group context should be achieved with the help of a 'group coordinator' (Article 71 EIR Recast), an independent person, whose main tasks consist of identifying and outlining recommendations for the coordinated conduct of the insolvency proceedings and drafting a group coordination plan (Article 72(1) EIR Recast). The group coordination plan may contain measures to re-establish the economic performance and the financial soundness of the group or any part of it, such as the increase of equity capital, simplification of the financial structure of the group, and the elimination of deficiencies in the intra-group cash pooling system. Measures might also aim to improve business performance, including through the reorganisation of the group structure, the realignment and refocusing of business activities, replacement of management, and personnel reduction.[109] Notably, the group coordination plan cannot include recommendations as to any consolidation of proceedings or insolvency estates (Article 72(3) EIR Recast).

The opening of a group coordination proceeding can be requested by an insolvency practitioner appointed in insolvency proceedings opened in relation to *any* group member, and before *any* court presiding over insolvency proceedings of a group member (Recital 55, Article 61 EIR Recast). Arguably, this can lead to a situation where a group coordination proceeding is opened in a jurisdiction unsuitable for a coordination task, whether due to language, economic or any other practical barriers. As a solution, Article 66 EIR Recast ('Choice of court for group coordination proceedings') allows insolvency practitioners appointed in insolvency proceedings of the members of the corporate group *by agreement* to choose the jurisdiction for the opening of group coordination proceedings, the courts of which shall have *exclusive* jurisdiction. This agreement requires participation (i.e. approval) of at least two-thirds of all insolvency practitioners appointed in insolvency proceedings of the members of the group. In this scenario, the court first seized of jurisdiction must decline its jurisdiction in favour of the chosen court (Article 66(3) EIR Recast). This is a fine example of a contractual insolvency forum selection.

One may rightfully object that coordination proceedings introduced in Chap. 5 EIR Recast are very different from 'normal' insolvency proceedings. Group coordination proceedings are voluntary in nature; they do not reflect 'insolvency', but 'coordination' and could therefore easily relate to any other economic activity. Members of the group are free to participate or not to participate in group coordinating proceedings. In addition, they lead to non-binding actions

---

[109] Wessels and Kokorin 2018, pp. 136–137.

(recommendations) of a group coordinator and the proposal of a group coordination plan setting out an integrated approach to the resolution of the group members' insolvencies.[110] As opposed to 'normal' insolvency proceedings, group coordination proceedings do not entail collective enforcement of creditors' claims and are closer to mediation in terms of the mode of operation. Despite these unique characteristics and important distinctions, group coordination proceedings strive to facilitate the effective administration of the insolvency proceedings of enterprise group members (Recital 57 EIR Recast). In this respect, they pursue a shared goal of maximising estate value in insolvency, either by way of a group-level restructuring (group wide solution) or through coordinated sale of the enterprise as a going concern.

To the extent that actions by insolvency practitioners may be classified as private, the possibility of them choosing the coordination jurisdiction by agreement is remarkable and highlights the private element in group insolvency. It also underscores the expansion of the use of private law mechanisms (consensual resolution of insolvency) in a traditionally court-centred insolvency and restructuring environment.

2.5 Conclusion

Corporate world is rapidly changing. New forms of business organisations are being developed, new ways to attract financing are being explored, and new types of business relations are being created. These changes can be viewed as intriguing challenges to conventional wisdom of (entrepreneurial) life, or as opportunities to make such life better and more efficient. Whichever opinion one may adhere to, law plays no small part in it. This chapter discusses one issue, namely allocation of the insolvency jurisdiction under the current European rules. Gradually formed throughout the 20th century, these rules culminated in the adoption of the EIR in 2000 and the EIR Recast in 2015. According to these instruments, international insolvency jurisdiction shall be determined by the presence of the debtor's centre of main interests (COMI), which is defined as the 'place where the debtor conducts the administration of its interests on a regular basis and which is ascertainable by third parties.'

The first part of the chapter (Sect. 2.3) introduces three situations or developments, which show that the concept of COMI, originating from the 1980s (if not earlier), does not seem to create legal certainty and cater to other needs of creditors and debtors.

---

[110] For these reasons, the new set of rules on group insolvency have had a mixed reception in legal literature, with the majority of authors expressing doubts as to their effectiveness and practical value, as well as to the high costs the group coordinating proceedings may bring with them and their complex character. See Thole and Dueñas 2015, pp. 214–227; Weiss 2015, pp. 192–213; Hess et al. 2018, p. 220; Wessels 2017, para 10929j.

The first situation concerns capital markets and the position of investors in them. The possibility to calculate investment risks underlies the European rules (e.g. EC Prospectus Directive), facilitating informed assessment of the assets and liabilities of the borrower, its financial position, profit and losses. However, the analysis of a selection of prospectuses indicates that insolvency forum and applicable insolvency rules in case of the borrower's insolvency, are frequently treated as an unpredictable event beyond parties' control. This result is unsatisfactory and can be partly attributed to the inherent indeterminacy of COMI and the impossibility of selecting it by consent. The second problem relates to insolvency of corporate groups. The approach adopted by the EIR Recast in this respect promotes the so-called entity-by-entity treatment. Accordingly, COMI of each group member is determined separately, with no or limited analysis of the group structure. This makes efficient group resolution (restructuring or sale of business as a going concern) less likely. The third challenge comes from technological advancement. The rise of the platform economy and platform-based businesses with little connection to any jurisdiction further complicates COMI determination. But even bigger disruption comes from decentralised business models, empowered by the application of the blockchain technology. While decentralised autonomous organisations, managed by dispersed holders of tokens, and algorithmic governance remain at the initial stage of development, the trend towards decentralisation should not be ignored. In the world of decentralised decision making, finding the place where the debtor conducts the administration of its interests becomes an impossible task.

These challenges set the scene for entering into a 'new age', which may require new solutions. The second part of the chapter (Sect. 2.4) analyses various tools being applied to customise the application of COMI. It should be noted that the present-day economic environment is quite different from that of the last quarter of the 20th century, the time in which modern insolvency law takes its roots. The creditors have become more professional and are now increasingly represented by sophisticated distressed asset managers. Another change comes from the proliferation of secured credit and an accompanying increase in the power of secured creditors in the insolvency process. This power goes beyond traditional voting rights and practically equates to contractually-created control over debtors' insolvency (thus, the term 'creditors in possession'). Other forms emanating from private law include restructuring support agreements and agreements accompanying rescue (debtor in possession) finance. These are examples of private (contractual) insolvency regulation of substantive character. The trend towards consensus-based resolution of financial distress is also supported by the Restructuring Directive, acknowledging the utility of limiting court involvement and adopting restructuring plans.

The question is whether the nascent shift to a contractual paradigm manifests itself in the treatment of international insolvency jurisdiction. The answer to this question draws on the analysis of three different practices, namely the contractual selection of the COMI-jurisdiction, synthetic and reverse synthetic insolvency proceedings, and selection of a group coordination forum. These solutions to the inherent ambiguity and fluidity of COMI may be used to construct (contract around) the insolvency jurisdiction, ensure efficient group resolution and well-functioning administration of the insolvency estate.

While the new tools offer an opportunity for creditors and other actors to alter the default COMI-option, they cannot and do not aim at replacing COMI or solving all the problems brought by the 'new age'. They may, however, indicate the emergence of an insolvency regime (partially) based on private ordering. The empowerment of private parties to engineer their own fate in insolvency scenarios fits well in the new world. The flexibility of contractual approaches can help addressing new enterprise forms and decentralised business models. They can also promote legal certainty and better calculation of market risk premiums. Synthetic/reverse synthetic proceedings and group coordination proceedings, currently underused, open the door for centralised and coordinated insolvency resolution in the context of corporate groups. Diverse forms of synthetic proceedings and the freedom to choose a group coordination forum under Article 66 EIR Recast are examples of institutionalised tools of *ex post* contracting. They can be used once insolvency proceeding(s) have been initiated. *Ex ante* contracting, that is contracting prior to insolvency, is less institutionalised and remains relatively marginal in Europe.

Acknowledgements I would like to express my gratitude to prof. em. Bob Wessels and Morshed Mannan, Ph.D. candidate at Leiden University, for helpful comments and discussions. The usual disclaimers apply.

References

4finance S.A. (2016) Prospectus dated 5 August 2016, ISIN XS1417876163, German Securities Identification Number (Wertpapierkennnummer WKN) A181ZP, Common Code 141787616. https://www.4finance.com/wp-content/uploads/2016/08/EUR-Bond-Listing-Prospectus.pdf. Accessed 1 June 2019

American Bankruptcy Institute (2014) ABI Commission to Study the Reform of Chapter 11, 2012–2014 Final Report and Recommendations. https://abiworld.app.box.com/s/vvircv5xv83aavl4dp4h. Accessed 1 June 2019

Anderson G et al (1983) The Economic Organization of the English East India Company. Journal of Economic Behavior and Organization 4:221–238

Aragon Network (2018) Aragon Network White Paper. https://github.com/aragon/whitepaper. Accessed 1 June 2019

Association of Corporate Treasurers (2008) Act borrower's guide to the LMA facilities agreement for leveraged transactions. https://www.treasurers.org/loandocumentation/leveraged. Accessed 1 June 2019

Baird D (2004) The New Face of Chapter 11. Am. Bankr. Inst. L. Rev. 12:69–99

Baird D (2016) Priority Matters: Absolute Priority, Relative Priority and the Costs of Bankruptcy. U. Penn L. Rev. 165(4):785–829

Baird D (2017) Bankruptcy's Quiet Revolution. Am. Bankr. L.J. 91:593–622

Bank for International Settlements, Basel Committee on Banking Supervision (2010) Report and Recommendations of the Cross-border Bank Resolution Group. http://www.bis.org/publ/bcbs169.htm. Accessed 1 June 2019

Berle A, Means G (1932) The Modern Corporation and Private Property. MacMillan, New York

Bufford S (2007) Center of Main Interests, International Insolvency Case Venue, and Equality of Arms: The Eurofood Decision of the European Court of Justice. Nw. J. Int'l L. & Bus. 27:351–420

Bufford S (2012) Coordination of Insolvency Cases for International Enterprise Groups: A Proposal. Am. Bankr. L.J. 86:685–748

Busch C (2019) Self-Regulation and Regulatory Intermediation in the Platform Economy. SSRN. In: Cantero Gamito M, Micklitz HW (forthcoming, 2019) The Role of the EU in Transnational Legal Ordering: Standards, Contracts and Codes. Edward Elgar

CERIL (2018) Realisation of the EU Insolvency Regulation (EIR 2015) in national (procedural) law of the Member States, CERIL Report 2018-1 on Insolvency Regulation (Recast) and National Procedural Rules. http://www.ceril.eu/news/realisation-of-the-eu-insolvency-regulation-eir-2015-in-national-procedural-law-of-the-member-states/. Accessed 1 June 2019

Colony (2018) Technical White Paper. https://colony.io/whitepaper.pdf. Accessed 1 June 2019

Dakin M et al (2012) Getting into bed with bondholders. Corporate Rescue and Insolvency, Clifford Chance 120–125

De Filippi P, Wright A (2018) Blockchain and the Law. The Rule of Code. Harvard University Press, Harvard

De Weijs R (2012) Harmonisation of European Insolvency Law and the Need to Tackle Two Common Problems: Common Pool and Anticommons. Int. Insolv. Rev. 21(2):67–83

Eidenmüller H (2005) Free Choice in International Company Insolvency Law in Europe. EBOR 6:423–447

Eidenmüller H (2009) Abuse of Law in the Context of European Insolvency Law. ECFR 6(1):1–28

Erikson E (2014) Between Monopoly and Free Trade: The English East India Company. Princeton University Press, Princeton

European Communities (Commission) (1982) Draft Convention on bankruptcy, winding-up, arrangements, compositions and similar proceedings. Report on the draft Convention. Bulletin of the European Communities, Supplement 2/82. http://aei.pitt.edu/5480/1/5480.pdf. Accessed 1 June 2019

Finch V, Milman D (2017) Corporate Insolvency Law: Perspectives and Principles, 3rd edn. Cambridge University Press, Cambridge

Finck M (2017) Digital Regulation: Designing a Supranational Legal Framework for Platform Economy. LSE Law, Society and Economy Working Papers 15/2017

Fletcher I (2005) Insolvency in Private International Law, 2nd edn. Oxford University Press, Oxford

Fletcher I (2016) Historical Overview: The Drafting of the Regulation and its Precursors. In: Moss G et al (ed), Moss, Fletcher and Isaacs on the EU Regulation on Insolvency Proceedings, 3rd edn. Oxford University Press, Oxford, paras 1.01–1.28

Georgakopoulos N (2017) The Logic of Securities Law. Cambridge University Press, Cambridge

Gilson R et al (2009) Contracting for Innovation: Vertical Disintegration and Interfirm Collaboration. Columbia Law Review 109(3):431–502

Goode R (2011) Principles of Corporate Insolvency Law, 4th edn. Sweet and Maxwell, London

Hamilton D, Hair S (2007) County Report – Great Britain. In: Pannen K (ed) European Insolvency Regulation: Commentary. De Gruyter Recht, Berlin, pp 635–666

Hess B et al (2018) The Implementation of the New Insolvency Regulation: Improving Cooperation and Mutual Trust. Nomos/Hart, Baden-Baden

INSOL International (2017) Directors in the Twilight Zone V

Jackson T (1982) Bankruptcy, Non-Bankruptcy Entitlements, and the Creditors' Bargain. Yale L. J. 91(5):857–907

Jackson T (1986) The Logic and Limits of Bankruptcy Law. Harvard University Press, Harvard

Keay A (2015) The Shifting of Directors' Duties in the Vicinity of Insolvency. Int. Insolv. Rev. 24 (2):140–164

Kokorin I (2017) The end of COMI as we know it: Insolvency rules in the era of decentralisation. Leiden Law Blog. https://leidenlawblog.nl/articles/the-end-of-comi-as-we-know-it-insolvency-rules-in-the-era-of-decentralisati. Accessed 1 June 2019

Kokorin I, Wessels B (2018) COMIs under Chapter 15 and EIR Recast: Brothers, but not Twins. ABI Journal, August 2018. https://abi-org-corp.s3.amazonaws.com/journals/european_08-18.pdf. Accessed 1 June 2019

Levitin A (2019) Business Bankruptcy: Financial Restructuring and Modern Commercial Markets, 2nd edn. Wolters Kluwer, New York

Madaus S (2018) Leaving the Shadows of US Bankruptcy Law: A Proposal to Divide the Realms of Insolvency and Restructuring Law. EBOR 19:615–647

Mannan M (2019) Fostering Worker Cooperatives with Blockchain Technology: Lessons from the Colony Project. Erasmus Law Review (forthcoming)

McCormack G (2009) Jurisdictional Competition and Forum Shopping in Insolvency Proceedings. Cambridge Law Journal 68(1):169–197

Mevorach I (2009) Insolvency within Multinational Enterprise Groups. Oxford University Press, Oxford

Millett P (1997) Cross-Border Insolvency: The Judicial Approach. Int. Insolv. Rev. 6(2):99–113

Morrison D, Anderson C (2013) The Australian Corporate Rescue Provisions: How do they Compare? In: Omar P (ed) International Insolvency Law: Reforms and Challenges. Ashgate, Farnham, pp 171–203

Moss G et al (2017) EU Banking and Insurance Insolvency, 2nd edn. Oxford University Press, Oxford

Nisi N (2017) The recast of the Insolvency Regulation: a third country perspective. J. Priv. Int. L. 13(2):324–355

Nocilla A (2017) Asset Sales and Secured Creditor Control in Restructuring: A Comparison of the UK, US and Canadian Models. Int. Insolv. Rev. 26:60–81

PETRONAS Capital Limited (2009) Prospectus dated 12 August 2009, International Securities Identification Number (ISIN) USY68856AH99, Common Code 044509822. https://data.cbonds.info/emissions/11521/Prospectus_Petronas_2019.pdf. Accessed 1 June 2019

Photon Energy N.V. (2017) Prospectus dated 21 September 2017, ISIN DE000A19MFH4

Pottow J (2011) A New Role for Secondary Proceedings in International Bankruptcies. Tex. Int'l L. J. 46(3):579–599

Ramesh K (2017) The Gibbs Principle: A Tether on the Feet of Good Forum Shopping. SAcLJ 29:42–74

Ramesh K (2018) Synthesising synthetics: Lessons learnt from Collins and Aikman, 2nd Annual GRR Live, New York

Rasmussen R (1992) Debtor's Choice: A Menu Approach to Corporate Bankruptcy. Texas L. Rev. 71:51–121

Rasmussen R (1997) A New Approach to Transnational Insolvencies. Mich. J. Int'l L. 19:1–36

Rasmussen R (2018) Taking Control Rights Seriously. U. Pa. L. Rev 166(1):1749–1776

Ringe WG (2017) Insolvency Forum Shopping, Revisited. Hamburg Law Review 3:38–59

Roe R (2017) Three Ages of Bankruptcy, Harvard Business Law Review 7:187–219

Schwartz A (1993) Bankruptcy Workouts and Debt Contracts. Journal of Law and Economics 36 (1):595–632

Schwartz A (2015) The Digital Shareholder. Minnesota Law Review 100(2):609–685

Siegel D (2016) Understanding the DAO Attack. https://www.coindesk.com/understanding-dao-hack-journalists. Accessed 1 June 2019

Simpson S, Goffman J (2011) Emergency Sales in the US and the UK. In: Mallon C, Waisman S (eds) The Law and Practice of Restructuring in the UK and US. Oxford University Press, Oxford, paras 2.01–2.98

Skeel D, Triantis G (2018) Bankruptcy's Uneasy Shift to a Contract Paradigm, Public Law and Legal Theory Research Paper Series. Research Paper 18–21

Squire R (2011) Strategic liability in the corporate group. U. Chi. L. Rev. 78:605–670

Stanghellini L et al (2018) Best Practices in European Restructuring. Contractualised Distress Resolution in the Shadow of the Law. Wolters Kluwer, Milan

Stilson A (1995) Re-examining the fiduciary paradigm at corporate insolvency and dissolution, defining directors' duties to creditors. Del. J. Corp. L. 20(1):1–122

Thole C, Dueñas M (2015) Some Observations on the New Group Coordination Procedure of the Reformed European Insolvency Regulation. Int. Insolv. Rev. 24(3):314–330

TUI AG (2016) Prospectus dated 21 October 2016, ISIN XS1504103984, Common Code 150410398, WKN A2BPFK. https://www.bourse.lu/security/XS1504103984/243417. Accessed 1 June 2019

Uber (2017) U.S. Terms of Use, Effective: 13 December 2017. https://www.uber.com/legal/terms/us/. Accessed 1 June 2019

UNCITRAL Working Group V (2018) Report on the fifty-fourth session (Vienna, 10–14 December 2018). https://undocs.org/pdf?symbol=en/A/CN.9/966. Accessed 1 June 2019

Virgós V, Schmit E (1996) Report on the Convention on Insolvency Proceedings. EU Council of the EU Document

Walthoff-Borm et al (2018) Equity crowdfunding, shareholder structures, and firm performance. Corporate Governance: An International Review 26(5):314–330

Weiss M (2015) Bridge over Troubled Water: The Revised Insolvency Regulation. Int. Insolv. Rev. 24(3): 192–213

Wessels B (2014) Contracting Out of Secondary Insolvency Proceedings: The Main Liquidator's Undertaking in Meaning of Article 18 in the Proposal to Amend the EU Insolvency Regulation. Brook. J. Corp. Fin. & Com. L. 9:63–110

Wessels B (2015) International Insolvency Law Part I. Global Perspectives on Cross-Border Insolvency Law. Wolters Kluwer, Deventer

Wessels B (2017) International Insolvency Law Part II – European Insolvency Law. Wolters Kluwer, Deventer

Wessels B, Kokorin I (2018) European Union Regulation on Insolvency Proceedings: An Introductory Analysis, 4th edn. American Bankruptcy Institute, Alexandria

World Bank (2016) Principles for Effective Insolvency and Creditor/debtor Regimes. http://documents.worldbank.org/curated/en/518861467086038847/Principles-for-effective-insolvency-and-creditor-and-debtor-regimes. Accessed 1 June 2019

Chapter 3
Jurisdictional Rules on Approval Requirements in the European Insolvency Regulation Recast

Julia Harten

Contents

Abstract This contribution deals with the rules on approval requirements in the European Insolvency Regulation Recast (EIR Recast) and argues that they are strengthening the role of the main insolvency proceedings. In many jurisdictions, current contracts of the debtor can be modified or terminated by the insolvency practitioner upon insolvency. In some jurisdictions, the modification or termination has to be approved by a court or a court-appointed supervisory judge. If the *lex fori concursus* does not contain the procedural rules to fulfil an approval requirement posed by the law applicable to the current contract in insolvency, an unintended regulatory gap exists. Articles 11(2) and 13(2) of the EIR Recast were introduced to solve this problem with regard to contracts relating to immoveable property and with regard to contracts of employment. Because the new provisions are reducing the need to open secondary proceedings, they are contributing to a more powerful role of the main insolvency proceedings.

J. Harten (✉)
Faculty of Law, University of Hamburg, Rothenbaumchaussee 33, 20148 Hamburg, Germany
e-mail: julia.harten@uni-hamburg.de

© T.M.C. ASSER PRESS and the authors 2020
V. Lazić and S. Stuij (eds.), *Recasting the Insolvency Regulation*, Short Studies in Private International Law,
https://doi.org/10.1007/978-94-6265-363-4_3

Keywords European Insolvency Regulation Recast · International insolvency law · Jurisdictional rules · Approval requirements · Main and secondary proceedings · Contracts relating to immoveable property · Contracts of employment · Adaptation

3.1 Introduction

The original European Insolvency Regulation[1] (hereinafter referred to as 'EIR') established within its scope of application uniform rules in international insolvency law.[2] Distinct from other prominent EU regulations, it contained rules on international jurisdiction, conflict of law rules, and a framework for the recognition and enforcement in other Member States. Therefore, it answered the three basic questions concerning the competent court, the applicable law, and the conditions for recognition and enforcement.[3] This chapter will deal with the first topic of international jurisdiction. More particularly, this contribution is devoted to the jurisdictional rules on approval requirements in international insolvency matters. The rules on these questions were added in the European Insolvency Regulation Recast of 2015[4] (hereinafter referred to as 'EIR Recast').

Overall, the EIR Recast maintained the core ideas of the EIR.[5] As for international jurisdiction, one main and several territorial or secondary proceedings can be opened.[6] The debtor's centre of main interests (COMI) determines the jurisdiction for the main proceeding.[7] Secondary proceedings can be opened in the Member States where the debtor has an establishment.[8] These are the basic rules which were already contained in the EIR. The general concepts of the COMI and the establishment were not changed.[9] However, the wording of the rules concerning the COMI was refined and additional rules were introduced.[10]

Articles 4 and 5 of the EIR Recast complement the functioning of the COMI, which remains regulated in Article 3 of the EIR Recast. Article 6 of the EIR Recast establishes the jurisdiction for actions related to the insolvency proceedings. Articles 11(2) and 13(2) of the EIR Recast contain new jurisdictional rules for

---

[1] Regulation (EC) 1346/2000 of 29 May 2000 on insolvency proceedings.

[2] Wessels 2011, p. 125.

[3] Bork 2017, p. 249; Wessels 2008, p. 70.

[4] Regulation (EU) 2015/848 of 20 May 2015 on insolvency proceedings (recast).

[5] Fletcher 2015, p. 98.

[6] Leandro 2014, p. 47.

[7] McCormack 2016, p. 129.

[8] Moss 2014, p. 11; for a detailed discussion of the establishment as a requirement to open secondary proceedings, see Bork and Harten 2018, pp. 673 et seq.

[9] Fletcher 2015, p. 99.

[10] Fletcher 2015, p. 99; Mucciarelli 2016, p. 13.

approval requirements under local law. This chapter focuses on the origin, purpose and role of the latter norms in the EIR Recast. It takes a look at their effect on the relationship between the main and the secondary proceedings.

The following section outlines the issue at stake and questions the need for a regulation of approval requirements in international insolvency law (Sect. 3.2). Afterwards, the newly added jurisdictional rules on approval requirements are introduced and analysed (Sect. 3.3). In this third section the consequences of the new rules on approval requirements for the functioning of the EIR Recast will also be scrutinised. It will be argued that the rules provide evidence for a strong role of the main insolvency proceeding to the detriment of the secondary proceedings. The last section concludes that the jurisdictional rules on approval requirements are contributing to a more powerful role of the main insolvency proceedings (Sect. 3.4).

3.2 The Issue: Approval Requirements in International Insolvency Law

In many jurisdictions, current contracts of the debtor can be modified or terminated by the insolvency practitioner upon insolvency.[11] In Germany, for example, Section 103 of the German Insolvency Code[12] gives the insolvency practitioner the options to perform or refuse the performance of a current contract.[13] In some jurisdictions, the modification or termination has to be approved by a court or a court appointed supervisory judge.[14] According to Article 64 of the Spanish Insolvency Act,[15] for example, the collective termination or modification of employment contracts requires a special court procedure.[16] However, in most

---

[11] Fletcher 2005, p. 414, para 7.108; Garcimartín 2015, p. 717; Piekenbrock 2014, p. 204, para 6.5.1; Veder 2011, p. 288.

[12] Section 103—Option to be exercised by the Insolvency Administrator—Insolvency Statute: '(1) Ist ein gegenseitiger Vertrag zur Zeit der Eröffnung des Insolvenzverfahrens vom Schuldner und vom anderen Teil nicht oder nicht vollständig erfüllt, so kann der Insolvenzverwalter anstelle des Schuldners den Vertrag erfüllen und die Erfüllung vom anderen Teil verlangen.

(2) Lehnt der Verwalter die Erfüllung ab, so kann der andere Teil eine Forderung wegen der Nichterfüllung nur als Insolvenzgläubiger geltend machen. Fordert der andere Teil den Verwalter zur Ausübung seines Wahlrechts auf, so hat der Verwalter unverzüglich zu erklären, ob er die Erfüllung verlangen will. Unterläßt er dies, so kann er auf der Erfüllung nicht bestehen' and see Section 113 Insolvency Statute for employment contracts.

[13] Paulus 2017, p. 278.

[14] Veder 2011, p. 288.

[15] Artículo 64—Contratos de trabajo—ley 22/2003, de 9 de julio, Concursal: 'Los expedientes de modificación sustancial de las condiciones de trabajo y de suspensión o extinción colectiva de las relaciones laborales, una vez declarado el concurso, se tramitarán ante el juez del concurso por las reglas establecidas en el presente artículo.'

[16] Garcimartín 2015, p. 717.

Member States no such court approval is necessary. This can create a problem of adaptation in international insolvency cases.[17] Generally, this problem arises, when two different national laws apply in one case and the combined result contradicts both of the involved national laws viewed separately.[18] In other words, the result was not intended by any of the involved national systems.[19] In general, in private international law, this problem can be solved by an adjustment of the rules in the individual case.[20]

The problem can occur in international insolvency law, when the applicable law requires a procedural element which is not provided for by the procedural law of the forum. If, for example, the debtor's COMI is in Germany, the main insolvency proceedings will be opened in Germany (Article 3(1) of the EIR Recast). In this case, German law is the law of the forum (*lex fori concursus*) and will be the applicable insolvency law (Article 7 of the EIR Recast). For current contracts, however, exceptions to the *lex fori concursus* are made. Articles 11 and 13 of the EIR Recast contain special rules for contracts relating to immoveable property and contracts of employment. To the contracts relating to immoveable property the law of the territory where the immoveable property is situated applies (Article 11(1) of the EIR Recast). To the effects of the insolvency proceedings on employment contracts the law that governs the contract of employment applies (Article 13(1) of the EIR Recast).

A problem arises when a main insolvency proceeding is opened in Germany and the debtor has employees in Spain under contracts of employment that are governed by Spanish law.[21] German insolvency law does not contain the same court procedure for the modification or termination as Spanish law. It is, therefore, questionable if and how the Spanish procedural requirements must and can be fulfilled. The first question, if the procedural elements have to be fulfilled, depends on the extent of the general rule for the applicable law with regard to its exceptions. The second question, how the procedural requirements could be fulfilled, has two possible answers: the foreign procedure could be carried out by the German courts which are conducting the main insolvency proceedings or by the Spanish courts which have a closer link to the required procedure.

The first question concerns the necessity to fulfil the procedural requirements of the law that governs the contract of employment. The answer depends on the scope of the general rule for the applicable law and its exceptions. Are the procedural aspects of the termination or modification of current contracts governed by the *lex fori concursus* (Article 7(2)(e) of the EIR Recast)? In this case, the foreign procedural requirements do not have to be fulfilled at all. Or are the procedural aspects contained in the clauses regulating the exceptions (Article 13(1) of the EIR Recast

---

[17] Garcimartín 2015, p. 716.

[18] Gössl 2018, p. 619.

[19] Gössl 2018, p. 619.

[20] Gössl 2018, pp. 622 et seq.

[21] See Garcimartín 2015, p. 716 for a similar example.

and respectively Article 11(1) of the EIR Recast)?[22] Only in this case, a problem of adaptation can arise, because the procedural requirements of another forum need to be fulfilled and this is not provided for by the law of the actual forum. After the amendment of the EIR through the EIR Recast, this question is not open for debate anymore. The additional rules show clearly that the procedural requirements are perceived to be contained in the rules governing the exceptions to the general rule. According to this interpretation, a regulatory gap that made an adaptation necessary existed before the amendment.

Thus, the second question has to be answered as well. It concerns the possibility to fulfil the procedural requirements which have no equivalent in the *lex fori concursus*. If the debtor has an establishment in Spain it is an option to open a secondary proceeding in Spain. If the debtor does not have an establishment in Spain, a secondary proceeding cannot be opened there. In the first case, the opening of a secondary proceeding might avoid the need for an adaptation but it leads to a costly and unnecessary secondary proceeding. In the latter case, it is unclear how the procedural requirement can be fulfilled. Hence, an adjustment could be necessary. A method of adjustment in private international law is the substitution.[23] In the case of a substitution, a requirement of a domestic or foreign rule is fulfilled within the scope of another law.[24] In the mentioned example, the Spanish approval requirement could be fulfilled by a German court. The Spanish rule is then adjusted to accept the German approval and the German rules are adjusted to accommodate the approval at its competent insolvency court.

In short, a problem only arises, because the procedural aspects of current contracts are perceived not to be contained in Article 7(2)(e) of the EIR Recast, but in the exceptions of Article 11 and Article 13 of the EIR Recast. This problem can be solved by the opening of a secondary proceeding if the debtor has an establishment in the relevant Member State. If there is no establishment in the relevant Member State an adjustment by the courts of the rules of the Member State that opened the main proceeding could have solved the problem. Therefore, new rules on approval requirements were not essentially needed. How they still came into force in the legislative history and their scope in the EIR Recast will be shown next.

3.3 Jurisdictional Rules on Approval Requirements

In the EIR Recast, two jurisdictional rules have now been added to provide a legislative solution for the regulatory problem that made an adaptation for current contracts necessary. These are Article 11(2) and Article 13(2) of the EIR Recast. They contain special provisions for approval requirements under local law. Article

---

[22] This question is also asked by Garcimartín and Virgós 2016, p. 278.
[23] Gössl 2018, p. 622; Looschelders 2019, para 1219.
[24] Gössl 2018, p. 622; Looschelders 2019, para 1219.

11(2) of the EIR Recast provides that '[the] court which opened main insolvency proceedings shall have jurisdiction to approve the termination or modification' of the contracts relating to immoveable property. This competence depends on two conditions: first, the law of the Member State that is applicable to the contract relating to immoveable property needs to contain an approval requirement for the termination or modification of the contract, and secondly, in that Member State no insolvency proceedings may have been opened.

Article 13(2) of the EIR Recast contains the rule for contracts of employment. It provides that: 'The courts of the Member State in which secondary insolvency proceedings may be opened shall retain jurisdiction to approve the termination or modification of the contracts referred to in this Article even if no insolvency proceedings have been opened in that Member State.' It further provides that the 'first subparagraph shall also apply to an authority competent under national law to approve the termination or modification of the contracts referred to in this Article.'

The following subsections are devoted to those two different rules on approval requirements. The first subsection describes the legislative development of the jurisdictional rules on approval requirements in the making of the EIR Recast (Sect. 3.3.1). The following second subsection analyses the purpose, functioning and consequences of Article 11(2) of the EIR Recast (Sect. 3.3.2). The third subsection examines Article 13(2) of the EIR Recast on the same grounds (Sect. 3.3.3). The final subsection summarises the previous findings and concludes that the new rules contribute to a readjustment of the relationship between the main and the secondary proceedings (Sect. 3.3.4).

3.3.1 Legislative Development

The legislative development of Articles 11(2) and 13(2) of the EIR Recast cannot be traced back to previous case law by the European Court of Justice. Their enactment was also not demanded or recommended by previous studies. Notably the Heidelberg-Luxembourg-Vienna Report,[25] which examined the original EIR, did not indicate a special need for legislative action concerning approval requirements. Regarding Article 8 of the EIR (which is now Article 11 of the EIR Recast) no amendments were recommended.[26] With respect to Article 10 of the EIR (which is now Article 13 of the EIR Recast) a greater need of reform was identified but no

[25] The Heidelberg-Luxembourg-Vienna Report on the Application of Regulation No. 1346/2000/EC on Insolvency Proceedings (External Evaluation JUST/2011/JCIV/PR/0049/A4) was presented by Hess B, Oberhammer P and Pfeiffer T in cooperation with Piekenbrock A and Seagon C in 2014.

[26] Piekenbrock 2014, p. 205, para 6.5.3: 'Therefore, we come to the conclusion that the choice of law rule is appropriate to meet the underlying policy and recommend no amendments.'

special amendment was proposed.[27] Indeed, concerning employment contracts, a few national reports identified possible fields of reform. The Spanish Report indicated a need for reform concerning the procedure of dismissal of employees that has to be observed under Spanish employment law.[28] The Dutch Report highlighted a qualification problem concerning approval requirements for the dismissal of employees.[29] Thus, in the field of employment contracts, there was at least a loose evidence for a need of reform.

A further insight into the development of Articles 11(2) and 13(2) of the EIR Recast is provided by the documents of the European legislative process. The material reveals that Articles 11(2) and 13(2) of the EIR Recast have a common root, even though they entail different legal consequences in their present form. Article 11(2) of the EIR Recast allocates the jurisdiction to approve the termination or modification of contracts relating to immoveable property to the court of the main proceedings. Article 13(2) of the EIR Recast assigns jurisdiction to approve the termination or modification of contracts of employment to the courts of the Member State where secondary proceedings may be opened.

In the original proposal of the European Commission, a combined rule was proposed, which assigned both approval requirements to the court of the main proceedings.[30] The wording of the proposed Article was as follows:

Where the law of the Member State governing the effects of insolvency proceedings on the contracts referred to in Articles 8 and 10 [of the original EIR] provides that a contract can only be terminated or modified with the approval of the court opening insolvency proceedings but no insolvency proceedings have been opened in that Member State, the court which opened the insolvency proceedings shall have the competence to approve the termination or modification of these contracts.[31]

This was approved by the European Parliament in the first instance[32] but discarded by the Council.[33] The proposed provision was split into two different paragraphs according to the contracts to which they are referring. Instead of adding a separate uniform article on approval requirements, the jurisdictional rules have now each been added as a second paragraph to the relevant provision. Article 11(2) of the EIR Recast provides a jurisdictional rule for the approval of the termination or modification of the contracts relating to immoveable property. Article 13(2) of the EIR

---

[27] Pfeiffer 2014, p. 206, para 6.7.1.1: 'Therefore, as a final conclusion in this respect, the General Reporters do not see differences in national labor laws as a sufficient reason for proposing an amendment of Article 10 EIR.'

[28] Pfeiffer 2014, p. 206, para 6.7.1.1.

[29] Pfeiffer 2014, p. 207, para 6.7.2.

[30] Article 10a proposal of the European Commission of 12.12.2012 (COM/2012/0744 final—2012/0360(COD)).

[31] Article 10a proposal of the European Commission of 12.12.2012 (COM/2012/0744 final—2012/0360(COD)).

[32] Position of the European Parliament adopted at first reading on 05.02.2014 (P7_TC1-COD (2012)0360), OJ C 93, 24.3.2017, p. 366.

[33] Position No. 7/2015 of the Council at first reading (2015/C-141/01), OJ C 141, 28.4.2015, p. 1.

Recast contains a rule on the jurisdiction to approve the termination or modification of contracts of employment.

Although the two paragraphs share a common root in the proposal of the European Commission, their final content differs significantly. According to Article 11(2) of the EIR Recast, the court which opened the main insolvency proceedings is competent for the approval, as it was originally proposed. Article 13(2) of the EIR Recast, however, determines that the courts of the Member State in which secondary proceedings could be opened have jurisdiction for the approval of the termination or the modification of employment contracts. Both paragraphs will be analysed in detail below.

3.3.2   Article 11(2) of the EIR Recast

Article 11(2) of the EIR Recast contains the provision on the jurisdiction for the approval of the termination or modification of contracts relating to immoveable property. Article 11(2) of the EIR Recast was inserted as a new paragraph in the updated regulation.[34] In the original EIR the provision on contracts relating to immoveable property was contained in Article 8 of the EIR. It concerned only the conflict of law question which law should govern the effects of insolvency proceedings on contracts 'conferring the right to acquire or make use of immoveable property'. In contrast to the general *lex fori concursus* rule of Article 4 of the EIR (now Article 7 of the EIR Recast) the 'law of the Member State within the territory of which the immoveable property is situated' should apply. This wording of para (1) was not changed in the EIR Recast.[35] The amendment only concerns Article 11 (2) of the EIR Recast. This subsection examines the purpose of the paragraph, its scope, and its impact on the applicable law.

3.3.2.1   Purpose

The purpose of Article 11 of the EIR Recast in general, is the protection of the local legal system[36] and the protection of the contractual partners of the debtor.[37] The details are not entirely clear, but their discussion is beyond the scope of this chapter. For the present purpose, it is sufficient to note the dual purpose that can be ascribed to the norm. It is based on the assumption that national legal orders concerning immoveable property differ significantly and it is difficult to give effect to judgements

---

[34] Kindler 2018a, p. 2066, para 10; Wenner and Schuster 2018a, p. 3518, para 12.
[35] Undritz 2017, p. 2485, para 7.
[36] Paulus 2017, p. 277; Reinhart 2016a, p. 137, para 1; Undritz 2017, p. 2484, para 1.
[37] Dornblüth 2018a, p. 2715, para 1.

on immoveable property if they contradict the law of the place of the property (*lex rei sitae*).[38]

The primary purpose of Article 11(2) of the EIR Recast is to close a gap in the original EIR.[39] As outlined above, this becomes relevant if the *lex rei sitae* requires a court approval for the modification or termination of a contract which is not provided for by the *lex fori concursus*. According to the original EIR, as well as the EIR Recast, a secondary proceeding can be opened in all Member States, where the debtor has an establishment. It is not sufficient for the opening of a secondary proceeding that the debtor has immoveable property in a Member State. Therefore, it is not always possible to open a secondary proceeding at the place of the immoveable property. In this case, another solution for the approval to terminations or modifications of contracts relating to immoveable property is necessary. The solution can be the competence of the court of the main insolvency proceedings. Even if a secondary proceeding could be opened at the place of the property, this could be costly and can be avoided if the court of the main proceedings is competent.[40]

The importance of Article 11(2) of the EIR Recast is not obvious. It is supposed to broaden the jurisdiction of the court of the main insolvency proceeding.[41] It has, however, also been argued that Article 11(2) of the EIR Recast has a declaratory function only, because Article 7(1) and (2) of the EIR Recast would produce the same result already.[42] This assertion is based on the assumption that Article 7(2)(e) of the EIR Recast includes the procedural aspects of the termination or modification of current contracts. The addition of Article 11(2) of the EIR Recast indicates, however, that the legislator perceived a need to clarify the issue.

Article 11(2) of the EIR Recast ascertains that the requirement of the foreign rule can be fulfilled through the courts and within the scope of the forum law. Originally, the foreign law that requires a court approval for the termination or modification of the contract, assumes the competence of the courts within the same jurisdiction for this approval. Article 11(2) of the EIR Recast enforces the acceptance of a foreign court as competent to conduct the required proceeding.[43] Furthermore, it ensures that the foreign court has the competence to conduct the proceeding. As has been explained above, this result could have been reached before the amendment with the instruments of private international law. In the literature, Article 11(2) of the EIR Recast is understood as a legally prescribed

---

[38] Snowden 2016, p. 264.

[39] Bork 2018a, para 16; Kindler 2018a, p. 2066, para 11; Wenner and Schuster 2018a, p. 3518, para 12.

[40] Kindler 2018a, p. 2066, para 11.

[41] Wenner and Schuster 2018a, p. 3517, para 2.

[42] Josko de Marx 2017, para 21.

[43] Mankowski 2016a, p. 253, para 44.

substitution in the law of the place of the property.[44] Such an adjustment of the foreign and domestic conflict of law rules and substantive law rules is an acknowledged method of private international law in various fields.[45] However, as long as the solution is not explicitly contained in the wording of the regulation, it could be disputed. Instead, it is now settled how the approval requirements can be fulfilled.

Thus, Article 11(2) of the EIR Recast prevents a further discussion of the jurisdictional competence in the area of contracts relating to immoveable property. The provision closes a potential gap in the EIR and it can make the opening of a secondary proceeding unnecessary.[46] This requires, however, that the case is within the scope of the provision.

3.3.2.2 Scope of the Jurisdiction

It is a prerequisite of Article 11(2)(b) of the EIR Recast that 'no insolvency proceedings have been opened in that Member State' where the immoveable property is situated. Thus, the jurisdictional rule in Article 11(2) of the EIR Recast is limited to cases where no secondary proceeding has been opened in the relevant Member State. This precondition is consistent. If a secondary proceeding is opened at the place of the property, this proceeding includes the property.[47] A problem creating the need for an adaptation does not arise, because the *lex rei sitae* is the law that is applicable in the secondary proceeding anyway.

If this condition is fulfilled, Article 11(2) of the EIR Recast provides an exclusive jurisdiction.[48] It regulates the international, territorial and material jurisdiction.[49] Hence, it is a direct allocation of jurisdiction for the court that opened the main insolvency proceedings.[50] A different agreement between the parties is not possible. This solution contains a definite deviation from the rules outside insolvency. According to Article 24 Nr. 1 of the Brussels Ibis Regulation,[51] outside insolvency the courts of the Member State in which the property is situated have exclusive jurisdiction for immovable property.[52]

---

[44] Mankowski 2016a, p. 253, para 44 ('Die eingesetzte Technik ist im kollisionsrechtlichen Sinne eine unionsrechtlich verordnete Substitution im Belegenheitsrecht.').

[45] Gössl 2018, pp. 618 et seq.

[46] Paulus 2017, p. 278; Snowden 2016, p. 266.

[47] Paulus 2017, p. 278.

[48] Wenner and Schuster 2018a, p. 3518, para 13.

[49] Garcimartín 2015, p. 718; Mankowski 2016a, p. 253, para 45.

[50] Paulus 2017, p. 278.

[51] Regulation (EU) No. 1215/2012 of the European Parliament and of the Council of 12 December 2012 on jurisdiction and the recognition and enforcement of judgments in civil and commercial matters.

[52] Mankowski 2016a, p. 253, para 43.

3.3.2.3 Impact on the Applicable Law

As a general rule in the EIR Recast, the *lex fori concursus* applies in the insolvency proceedings. Therefore, any change to the jurisdictional rules has a possible impact on the applicable law as well. This is not true for Article 11(2) of the EIR Recast. The provision complements Article 11(1) of the EIR Recast and does not contain a counter-exception to it. The court of the main insolvency proceeding, therefore, has to apply foreign law.[53] Article 11(2) of the EIR Recast even enforces this result by ensuring that the court has the necessary jurisdiction.

3.3.3 Article 13(2) of the EIR Recast

Article 13 of the EIR Recast concerns contracts of employment. Article 13(1) of the EIR Recast contains a choice of law provision that establishes an exception to the general rule of Article 7 of the EIR Recast.[54] According to Article 13(1) of the EIR Recast, the law that governs the contract of employment shall govern the effects of the insolvency proceedings on employment contracts, instead of the *lex fori concursus*. This rule was already contained in Article 10 of the original EIR; the wording has not changed.[55] However, as outlined above, Article 13(2) of the EIR Recast was inserted as a new paragraph in the reform process.[56] The norm is similar to Article 11(2) of the EIR Recast, but entails different legal consequences. It provides that the 'courts of the Member State in which secondary proceedings could be opened shall retain jurisdiction' for the approval requirements, even if no secondary proceedings were opened. This subsection outlines the purpose and the scope of Article 13(2) of the EIR Recast as well as its impact on the applicable law.

3.3.3.1 Purpose

The purpose of Article 13 of the EIR Recast is the protection of employees in case of the insolvency of the employer.[57] The employees shall be safeguarded from the application of a different law.[58] Thereby, a problem can occur, when the law that governs the effects of the insolvency on the employment contract requires a court

---

[53] Snowden 2016, p. 266; Wenner and Schuster 2018a, p. 3518, para 14.

[54] Garcimartín and Virgós 2016, p. 274.

[55] Dornblüth 2018b, p. 2718, para 1; Garcimartín and Virgós 2016, p. 275; Kindler 2018b, p. 2069, para 1.

[56] Liersch 2017, p. 289, para 17.

[57] Mankowski 2016b, p. 266, para 3; Paulus 2017, p. 284; Wenner and Schuster 2018b, p. 3520, para 1.

[58] Mankowski 2016b, p. 266, para 2; Garcimartín and Virgós 2016, p. 274.

approval for the termination or modification of employment contracts upon insolvency.[59] Article 13(2) of the EIR Recast was inserted to solve this problem with a prescribed adaptation[60] and to close a gap in the original EIR.[61]

In a broader perspective, however, Article 13(2) of the EIR was inserted to avoid the opening of secondary proceedings.[62] In the field of employment law, different levels of protection against dismissal exist in the Member States. For employers, it became attractive to relocate their COMI to the Member States with a low standard of employment protection.[63] For employees, on the other hand, it became appealing to open a secondary proceeding to benefit of stronger protection against dismissal.[64] This combination of incentives led to costly openings of secondary proceedings. This shall be avoided by Article 13(2) of the EIR Recast.[65]

3.3.3.2 Scope of the Jurisdiction

Whether Article 13(2) of the EIR Recast closes the gap for all relevant cases depends on the interpretation of the paragraph. According to a strict formal interpretation, Article 13(2) of the EIR Recast only applies in situations where secondary proceedings could be opened. Following this understanding of the paragraph, when secondary proceedings cannot be opened, because the debtor has no establishment in the relevant Member State, the jurisdictional rule would not be of any avail. According to this interpretation, a gap still remains in the EIR Recast.[66] This gap would still have to be closed by the traditional methods of private international law.

In order to close this gap in accordance with the legislative changes, an analogous application of the norm is supported instead.[67] This solution of an analogous

---

[59] Mankowski 2016b, p. 278, para 40 argues that the approval requirements of the Member State where a secondary proceeding could be opened are decisive, rather than the approval requirements of the law that governs the employment contract—if this is true a problem of adaptation does not exist because the law that governs the secondary proceeding does not apply in the main proceeding; for the decisiveness of the law that governs the employment contract, see Bork 2018b, para 16 and Paulus 2017, p. 290—the latter opinion is, however, problematic when the law that governs the contract of employment is not the law of the forum of the potential secondary proceeding. In that case, the same problem of adaptation can occur in the secondary proceeding, which might not necessarily have the same approval requirements as the law that governs the employment contract.

[60] Garcimartín and Virgós 2016, p. 278.

[61] Bork 2018b, para 16; Liersch 2017, p. 289, para 17.

[62] Kindler 2018b, p. 2071, para 13; Mankowski 2016b, p. 277, para 35; Wenner and Schuster 2018b, p. 3522, para 8.

[63] Mankowski 2016b, p. 277, para 35.

[64] Mankowski 2016b, p. 277, para 35.

[65] Wenner and Schuster 2018b, p. 3522, para 8.

[66] Liersch 2017, p. 290, para 18.

[67] Bork 2018b, para 18; Dornblüth 2018b, p. 2720, para 6; Reinhart 2016b, p. 425, para 4.

application is preferable. The purpose of the norm is to close a gap in the regulation. The decisive elements which characterise this gap are the diverging provisions for the applicable substantive law and the applicable procedural law. As long as no secondary proceeding is opened the applicable substantive and procedural law do not depend on the presence of an establishment. The situation without an establishment is comparable to the situation with an establishment. Therefore, all cases in which no secondary proceeding is opened should be treated equally. Hence, an interpretation of the new rule that closes the gap completely is preferable.

3.3.3.3 Impact on the Applicable Law

Article 13(2) of the EIR Recast does not change the law that is applicable to the employment contract.[68] Hence, the competent court has to apply the law designated by Article 13(1) of the EIR Recast. This outcome is based on an understanding of Article 13(2) of the EIR Recast as a purely jurisdictional rule and not a choice of law rule.[69] Article 13(2) of the EIR Recast, therefore, underlines the exception to the applicable law for employment contracts on the level of the international jurisdiction.

3.3.4 Consequences of the New Rules on Approval Requirements

Article 11(2) and Article 13(2) of the EIR Recast are jurisdictional rules. They are applicable in specific circumstances only. However, they have broader consequences for the understanding of the functioning of the EIR Recast. This subsection summarises the previous findings and argues that the rules on the approval requirements contribute to a readjustment of the relationship between the main and the secondary proceedings.

Both of the considered provisions are jurisdictional rules. They are no choice of law rules. Nevertheless, they do have an effect on the applicable law. Article 11(2) of the EIR Recast enhances the applicability of the *lex rei sitae*, because it enables the courts of the main insolvency proceedings to fulfil the requirements of the *lex rei sitae*.[70] Also, Article 13(2) of the EIR Recast perpetuates the exception to the *lex fori concursus*, because it facilitates the application of a foreign law. This is detrimental for a uniform application of one set of norms.

---

[68] Bork 2016, p. 153, para 4.96.
[69] Bork 2016, p. 153, para 4.96.
[70] Bork 2016, p. 149, para 4.84.

On the other hand, the norms have an influence on the relationship between the main and the secondary proceedings.[71] Article 11(2) of the EIR Recast is useful for the main proceedings.[72] It strengthens the proceedings at the COMI and reduces the reasons to open secondary proceedings.[73] Thus, it can avoid a partitioning of the proceedings. Article 13(2) of the EIR Recast has a weaker effect. It does not directly strengthen the main proceedings through additional competences. However, it also reduces the incentives to open secondary proceedings. Accordingly, it has an indirect strengthening effect on the main proceedings. The main proceedings are not directly granted further power, but they retain more power if less secondary proceedings are opened. This reveals the underlying purpose of the amendment. The new rules for approval requirements are contributing to a rearrangement of main and secondary proceedings. They are strengthening the main proceeding.

3.4   Conclusion

Articles 11(2) and 13(2) of the EIR Recast contain new jurisdictional rules on approval requirements. The primary purpose of those rules is the improvement of the functioning of the EIR. Their goal was to close an unintended gap in the original EIR with regard to contracts relating to immoveable property and contracts of employment. This problem could, however, also have been solved with the traditional methods of private international law through an adaptation.

At the same time, the development of the provisions cannot be traced back to extensive case law. It has been shown that their enactment can rather be seen as a response to the extensive use of secondary proceedings. The underlying purpose of the provisions is a strengthening of the main insolvency proceeding at the COMI and the avoidance of secondary proceedings at the establishment.

Some details of both norms are not entirely clear. With a view to the historically scarce court decisions in this area, this might not lead to practical problems which could produce significant decisions in the future. Overall, it can be expected that the practical impact of the rules on approval requirements will be minor. Nevertheless, the provisions are providing a signal for the rearrangement of the relationship between the main and the secondary proceedings. They are strengthening the main proceedings.

---

[71] For general comments on the relationship, see Moss 2014, p. 11; Wessels 2014, p. 23.
[72] Snowden 2016, p. 266.
[73] Snowden 2016, p. 266.

References

Bork R (2016) Law Applicable. In: Bork R, Mangano R (eds) European Cross-Border Insolvency Law. Oxford University Press, Oxford, pp 115–166

Bork R (2017) The European Insolvency Regulation and the UNCITRAL Model Law on Cross-Border Insolvency. International Insolvency Review 26:246–269

Bork R (2018a) Artikel 11 Vertrag über einen unbeweglichen Gegenstand. In: Kübler B et al (eds) InsO - Kommentar zur Insolvenzordnung, 77. Aktualisierung. RWS, Cologne, pp 1–7

Bork R (2018b) Artikel 13 Arbeitsvertrag. In: Kübler B et al (eds) InsO - Kommentar zur Insolvenzordnung, 77. Aktualisierung. RWS, Cologne, pp 1–8

Bork R, Harten J (2018) Die Niederlassung iSv Art. 2 Nr. 10 EuInsVO bei natürlichen Personen. Neue Zeitschrift für Insolvenz- und Sanierungsrecht 2018:673–680

Dornblüth S (2018a) Artikel 11 Vertrag über einen unbeweglichen Gegenstand. In: Kayser G, Thole C (eds) Heidelberger Kommentar zur Insolvenzordnung, 9th edn. C. F. Müller, Heidelberg, pp 2714–2716

Dornblüth S (2018b) Artikel 13 Arbeitsvertrag. In: Kayser G, Thole C (eds) Heidelberger Kommentar zur Insolvenzordnung, 9th edn. C. F. Müller, Heidelberg, pp 2718–2720

Fletcher I (2005) Insolvency in Private International Law, 2nd edn. Oxford University Press, Oxford

Fletcher I (2015) The European Insolvency Regulation recast: the main features of the new law. Insolvency Intelligence 28:97–103

Garcimartín F (2015) The EU Insolvency Regulation Recast: Scope, Jurisdiction and Applicable Law. Zeitschrift für Europäisches Privatrecht 23:694–731

Garcimartín F, Virgós M (2016) Article 13 – Contracts of employment. In: Bork R, van Zwieten K (eds) Commentary on the European Insolvency Regulation. Oxford University Press, Oxford, pp 274–279

Gössl S (2018) Anpassung im EU-Kollisionsrecht. Rabels Zeitschrift für ausländisches und internationales Privatrecht 82:618–653

Josko de Marx A (2017) Art. 11 Vertrag über einen unbeweglichen Gegenstand. In: Braun E (ed) Insolvenzordnung (InsO), 7th edn. C.H. Beck, Munich

Kindler P (2018a) Art. 11 EuInsVO Vertrag über einen unbeweglichen Gegenstand. In: Säcker F et al (eds) Münchener Kommentar zum Bürgerlichen Gesetzbuch, Band 12, 7th edn. C.H. Beck, Munich, pp 2063–2066

Kindler P (2018b) Art. 13 EuInsVO Arbeitsvertrag. In: Säcker F et al (eds) Münchener Kommentar zum Bürgerlichen Gesetzbuch, Band 12, 7th edn. C.H. Beck, Munich, pp 2069–2072

Leandro A (2014) Strengthening the Dominance of Main Proceedings: From Bank Handlowy to the Revision of the European Insolvency Regulation. In: Bariatti S, Omar P (eds) The Grand Project: Reform of the European Insolvency Regulation. INSOL Europe, Nottingham/Paris, pp 47–57

Liersch O (2017) Artikel 13 Arbeitsvertrag. In: Vallender H (ed) EuInsVO – Kommentar zur Verordnung (EU) 2015/848 über Insolvenzverfahren. RWS, Cologne, pp 285–290

Looschelders D (2019) Einleitung zum Internationalen Privatrecht. In: Henrich D (ed) J von Staudingers Kommentar zum Bürgerlichen Gesetzbuch mit Einführungsgesetz und Nebengesetzen, 2019. Sellier – de Gruyter, Berlin, pp 1–511

Mankowski P (2016a) Art. 11 Vertrag über einen unbeweglichen Gegenstand. In: Mankowski P et al (eds) Europäische Insolvenzverordnung 2015 – Kommentar, 1st edn. C.H. Beck, Munich, pp 241–254

Mankowski P (2016b) Art. 13 Arbeitsvertrag. In: Mankowski P et al (eds) Europäische Insolvenzverordnung 2015 – Kommentar, 1st edn. C.H. Beck, Munich, pp 265–278

McCormack G (2016) Something Old, Something New: Recasting the European Insolvency Regulation. The Modern Law Review 79:121–146

Moss G (2014) Master and Servant? Relationship between Main and Territorial Proceedings in Light of Bank Handlowy (Case C-116/11). In: Bariatti S, Omar P (eds) The Grand Project: Reform of the European Insolvency Regulation. INSOL Europe, Nottingham/Paris, pp 11–16

Mucciarelli F (2016) Private International Law Rules in the Insolvency Regulation Recast: A Reform or a Restatement of the Status Quo? European Company and Financial Law Review 13:1–30

Paulus C (2017) EuInsVO - Europäische Insolvenzverordnung, 5th edn. Fachmedien Recht und Wirtschaft, dfv Mediengruppe, Frankfurt am Main

Pfeiffer T (2014) Article 10 EIR: Employment Contracts. In: Hess B et al (eds) European Insolvency Law – The Heidelberg-Luxembourg-Vienna Report on the Application of Regulation No. 1346/2000/EC on Insolvency Proceedings (External Evaluation JUST/2011/ JCIV/PR/0049/A4). C. H. Beck/Hart/Nomos, Munich/Oxford/Baden-Baden, pp 206–208

Piekenbrock A (2014) Article 8 EIR: Contracts Relating to Immoveable Property. In: Hess B et al (eds) European Insolvency Law – The Heidelberg-Luxembourg-Vienna Report on the Application of Regulation No. 1346/2000/EC on Insolvency Proceedings (External Evaluation JUST/2011/JCIV/PR/0049/A4). C. H. Beck/Hart/Nomos, Munich/Oxford/Baden-Baden, pp 204–205

Reinhart S (2016a) Art. 8 Vertrag über einen unbeweglichen Gegenstand. In: Kirchhof H et al (eds) Münchener Kommentar zur Insolvenzordnung, 3rd edn. C. H. Beck, Munich, pp 137–142

Reinhart S (2016b) Art. 13 Arbeitsvertrag. In: Kirchhof H et al (eds) Münchener Kommentar zur Insolvenzordnung, 3rd edn. C. H. Beck, Munich, pp 424–425

Snowden R (2016) Article 11 – Contracts relating to immoveable property. In: Bork R, van Zwieten K (eds) Commentary on the European Insolvency Regulation. Oxford University Press, Oxford, pp 264–266

Undritz S (2017) Art. 8 Vertrag über einen unbeweglichen Gegenstand. In: Schmidt A (ed) Hamburger Kommentar zum Insolvenzrecht, 6th edn. Carl Heymanns, Cologne, pp 2484–2485

Veder M (2011) The Future of the European Insolvency Regulation – Applicable law, in particular security rights. International Insolvency Law Review 2:285–297

Wenner C, Schuster M (2018a) Artikel 11 Vertrag über einen unbeweglichen Gegenstand. In: Wimmer K (ed) Frankfurter Kommentar zur Insolvenzordnung mit EuInsVO, InsVV und weiteren Nebengesetzen, 9th edn. Luchterhand, Cologne, pp 3516–3518

Wenner C, Schuster M (2018b) Artikel 13 Arbeitsvertrag. In: Wimmer K (ed) Frankfurter Kommentar zur Insolvenzordnung mit EuInsVO, InsVV und weiteren Nebengesetzen, 9th edn. Luchterhand, Cologne, pp 3520–3522

Wessels B (2008) Cross-Border Insolvency Law in Europe: Present Status and Future Prospects. Potchefstroom Electronic Law Journal 11:68–102

Wessels B (2011) Amending the EU Insolvency Regulation: Shaken or Stirred? In: Parry R (ed) The Reform of International Insolvency Rules at European and National Level. INSOL Europe, Nottingham/Paris, pp 125–135

Wessels B (2014) Courts should be Leading in Solving Cross-Border Insolvency Matters. In: Bariatti S, Omar P (eds) The Grand Project: Reform of the European Insolvency Regulation. INSOL Europe, Nottingham/Paris, pp 23–31

Chapter 4
The Law Applicable to Transaction Avoidance in Cross-Border Insolvency Proceedings

Elena-Alina Oprea

Contents

Abstract   The possibility to set aside the detrimental transactions or acts concluded by the (insolvent) debtor prior to the opening of insolvency proceedings is widely recognised in comparative law. Given, the significant divergences existing between the substantive legislations as regards the prerequisites for and the boundaries for the avoidance actions, the solution for the conflicts of laws is a major issue. The chapter reviews the legal norms consecrated by the European Insolvency Regulation(s) in the field, trying to assess their aptitude to sustain the objectives

E.-A. Oprea (✉)
Faculty of Law, Babes-Bolyai University, Cluj-Napoca, Romania
e-mail: alina.oprea@law.ubbcluj.ro

© T.M.C. ASSER PRESS and the authors 2020
V. Lazić and S. Stuij (eds.), *Recasting the Insolvency Regulation*, Short Studies in Private International Law,
https://doi.org/10.1007/978-94-6265-363-4_4

followed by the European legislator: stability, coherence and reduction, at least in part, of the costs generated by the international character of the disputes. Through an analysis of the European Court of Justice's pertinent case law, the chapter highlights the difficulties and inconveniences raised by the complex articulation between *lex concursus* and *lex causae* and advances short proposals on the possible remedies that might be implemented in the future in this field.

Keywords cross-border insolvency proceedings · *actio pauliana* · *lex concursus* · *lex causae* · ECJ case law · harmonisation

4.1 Introductory Aspects—*Actio Pauliana*

Among the solutions consecrated for the protection of credit in insolvency proceedings, an important role is played by the possibility to set aside some transactions or acts concluded prior to the opening of insolvency that turn out to be detrimental to creditors' interests.

Inspired by the famous *actio pauliana* of the Roman law,[1] the transactions avoidance laws are based upon the principle of equal treatment of creditors. They generally aim to ensure the equitable treatment of creditors in the proceedings, to increase the chances of the business rescue through a maximisation of the value of the insolvency estate or to sanction the possible frauds committed by the debtor in detriment of its creditors. To this effect, they provide the right for the insolvency practitioner to take legal action against a third party and to obtain the avoidance of some transactions which, at the time of their conclusion and on the opening of the insolvency proceedings, were most likely valid and could not be challenged on the basis of the ordinary rules of Civil or Commercial Law.[2] Because the transactions avoidance goes against the third party's expectations, has important social costs and may affect the general solidity of trade, the States pay equal attention to the protection of trust in the stability and continuity of the acquired rights on their territories and set particular substantive prerequisites and boundaries for avoidance actions. The articulation of the principles of equal treatment of creditors and protection of trust is a delicate issue and comparative law illustrates very different solutions as regards the balance between the different interests at stake.[3]

---

[1] Pretelli 2011, p. 591; Bork 2017.

[2] See UNCITRAL Legislative Guide on Insolvency Law 2004; Keay 2017, part II; Gurrea-Martínez 2018.

[3] For an overview of the disparities existing among the EU Member States' legislations in this field, see McCormack et al. 2016, pp. 141 et seq. See also Carballo Piñeiro 2014, p. 212.

4.1.1   Uniform Rules in European Insolvency Regulation(s)

At the European Union level, with regard to the cross-border insolvencies, the Regulation 1346/2000 (EIR), now replaced by Regulation 2015/848 (EIR Recast), established uniform rules on the jurisdiction, the applicable law and the recognition of judgments.[4] Their purpose is to enable the effective and efficient operation of the proceedings, by ensuring the stability and the coherence, reducing *forum shopping* and limiting, at least partially, the costs generated by the cross-border nature of the cases.

4.1.1.1   Jurisdiction for *Actio Pauliana*

According to the Article 3 EIR Recast, the courts of the Member State within the territory of which the centre of main interests ('COMI') of a debtor is located have jurisdiction to open insolvency proceedings. In its case law, the European Court of Justice acknowledged the principle of *vis attractiva concursus* and stated that the courts of the debtor's COMI will also have jurisdiction to decide an action to set a transaction aside by virtue of insolvency (avoidance action or *actio pauliana*), regardless whether it is brought against a person whose registered office (or place of residence) is located in another Member State[5] or in a third State.[6] Article 6(1) EIR Recast expressly confirms this principle nowadays.

---

[4] Regulation (EC) no. 1346/2000 of the Council of 29 May 2000 *on insolvency proceedings* (OJ L 160, 30.6.2000, p. 1) (in the following, it will be cited as Regulation 1346/2000 or EIR). It was repealed and replaced by EU Regulation 2015/848 of 20 May 2015 *on insolvency proceedings* (OJ L 141, 5.6.2015), applicable to insolvency proceedings opened from June 26, 2017. The Regulations do not apply to the insolvency of entities like insurance undertakings, credit institutions, investment undertakings which provide services involving the holding of funds or securities for third parties, collective investment undertakings (Article 1(2)). Even if they contain also an important set of substantial norms (mainly as regards the situation of creditors), the Regulations do not attempt to generally unify or harmonise substantive laws of the Member States in the field of insolvency.

[5] ECJ 12.2.2009—Case C-339/07 (*Chr. Seagon v. Deko Marty Belgium*); Carballo Pinero 2010, pp. 1 et seq.

[6] ECJ 16.1.2014—Case C-328/12 (*R. Schmid*). Some doubts about the persistence of this solution are possible after the adoption of EIR Recast, since the Recital 35 from its Preamble speaks about the jurisdiction of Member States courts to decide avoidance actions '*against defendants in other Member States*'. Despite the direct opposition with the *Schmid* judgment, we do not think that this last judgment should be considered as reversed. Article 6 EIR Recast—the only provision with mandatory effect—does not require the domicile of the defendant within EU for the EIR Recast to apply. Moreover, the solution in *Schmid* has been reaffirmed by the ECJ not only prior to the adoption of the EIR Recast (see ECJ 4.12.2014—Case C-285/13, *H*, para 33), but also afterwards (see ECJ 11.06.2015—Case C-649/13, *Nortel*). Also, the arguments advanced by the Court are still actual for the interpretation and application of the EIR Recast.

4.1.1.2 Law Governing Collective Avoidance Actions

Pursuant to Article 7(2)(m) EIR Recast (former Article 4(2)(m) EIR), the law of the Member State where the insolvency proceedings were opened (*lex concursus*) will establish the substantive rules[7] which determine the voidness, voidability or unenforceability of legal acts detrimental to the general body of creditors. This choice of law rule gives proper consideration to the fact that the (collective) avoidance actions are closely connected to the insolvency proceedings and they facilitate the realisation of the insolvency proceedings' purposes. Article 7(2)(m) ensures a consistent and unitary treatment of the procedure and of the creditors, who will all be subject to the same law, *lex concursus*, as regards the voidness, voidability or unenforceability of the legal acts concluded with the debtor. It has strong justifications. The application of a single law as regards the different (challengeable) acts concluded by the insolvent debtor with various third parties is able to ease the mission of the insolvency practitioner.[8] As well, such a solution may dissuade the debtor from displacing some of its assets on the territory of other States than the one of its COMI, because the *lex concursus* will have a universal reach and, in principle, its avoidance provisions will have to be followed whatever the location of those assets would be.

Through express derogations, the rule established in Article 7(2)(m) will prevail over the special provisions from Articles 8(1), 9(1) and 10(1)–(2) EIR Recast. Thus, the *lex concursus* will also be considered as regards the avoidance actions of the rights *in rem* of creditors or third parties in respect of tangible or intangible, moveable or immoveable assets, both specific assets and collections of indefinite assets as a whole which change from time to time,[9] as regards the avoidance actions of the contracts that generate obligations for which a set-off will be demanded in the proceedings[10] or for the avoidance actions of the contracts providing for an eventual reservation of title.[11] Although it (also) favours the maximisation of the debtor's estate, this solution seeks to ensure that the rights protected by those articles, and subject to a special regime, were in fact validly created or acquired. It reflects the willingness of the European legislator to prevent the harm of the collective interests of the creditors through some acts concluded prior to the opening of the insolvency proceedings and that would benefit from the special and more

---

[7] Presumably, renvoi is excluded; see Recital 66 from the Preamble, stating that '*for the matters covered by it, uniform rules on conflict of laws which replace, within their scope of application, national rules of private international law; unless otherwise stated, the law of the Member State of the opening of proceedings should be applicable*'.

[8] This affirmation must be relativized: as it will be shown *infra* (paras 2.3 et seq), the *lex concursus* provisions regarding the avoidance of detrimental transactions are not the only provisions to which the insolvency practitioner must obey, and this will increase both the difficulty of its mission and the uncertainties as regards the success of its attempts.

[9] Article 8(4) EIR Recast.

[10] Article 9(2) EIR Recast.

[11] Article 10(3) EIR Recast.

favourable regime established by the laws (different from *lex concursus*) designated by these special conflicts of laws rules. This last idea also explains why no attempts of modification of the solution were made during the recast process.

4.1.1.3 Scope of *Lex Concursus*

As regards the avoidance actions, the *lex concursus* has a broad scope of application. It will determine the range of transactions susceptible of avoidance (transactions defrauding the creditors, transactions at an undervalue, payments made before the due date, payments made by unusual means, collaterals for pre-existing debts, transactions involving related persons[12]), the duration of the suspect period and its beginning, the substantive prerequisites for the avoidance, the standing to bring avoidance actions, the way in which the avoidance operates (by force of law, by declaration of the insolvency practitioner or by court decision[13]), the available defences, the procedural steps which must be taken into account for the invalidation of the act, the presumptions and the burden of proof. Furthermore, the *lex concursus* will be considered as well as regards the consequences of the avoidance (restitution of the payments made or of the transferred assets, payment of a compensation and/ or of interests) and all other effects of the relationship between the parties (although they could have been previously governed by another law). If the *lex concursus* does not allow the transaction's avoidance, this will not be set aside even if the

---

[12] For clarifications from this point of view, see ECJ 10.12.2015—Case C-594/14 (*Kornhaas*) in which the European Court of Justice was seised for a preliminary ruling regarding the characterisation of a legal situation involving the applicability of the provisions of the German Law on limited liability companies (that obliges the managing directors to reimburse the company with any payments made on behalf of the company after it became insolvent or was established that it was over-indebted). The Court considered that national provisions which have the effect, in essence, of penalising a failure to fulfil the obligation to apply for the opening of insolvency proceedings, must be considered to fall within the scope of Article 4 EIR (now Article 7 EIR Recast). Considering the aim of the national provision at issue (it contributes to the attainment of an objective which is intrinsically linked, *mutatis mutandis*, to all insolvency proceedings, namely the prevention of any reduction of the assets of the insolvent estate before the insolvency proceedings are opened, so that the claims of all the company's creditors may be satisfied on equal terms), the Court ruled that such a provision '*appears at least similar to a rule laying down the 'unenforceability of legal acts detrimental to all the creditors' which, under Article 4(2)(m) of Regulation No 1346/2000, comes within the lex fori concursus*' (para 20).

[13] This is an aspect already clarified by the ECJ in its judgment *Lutz* (ECJ 16.4.2015—Case C-557/13, detailed infra, para 3.1) in regard with the precision found in the majority of language versions of Article 5(4) EIR, submitting to the *lex concursus* the '*actions*' for voidness, voidability or unenforceability of rights *in rem*. The Court considered that Article 5(4) EIR should be read in conjunction with Article 4(2)(m) EIR, which is drafted in more general terms, and stated that: '*in order to determine whether the voidness, voidability or unenforceability of an act may result from legal action, from another legal measure or even from the effect of law, reference should be made to the competent lex fori concursus for determining, in accordance with Article 4(2)(m) of Regulation No 1346/2000, the rules relating to voidness, voidability or unenforceability*' (para 30).

insolvency provisions of the State whose law governs that transaction would provide for a different solution.[14]

Despite this apparently simple presentation, many intricacies appear in practice. Their source is found in the exceptions and derogations set by that the European legislator to the intervention of the *lex fori concursus*. The European Court of Justice's indications in its recent case law reveal both the amplitude of the existing difficulties and the departure from the general objectives announced in this field by the European legislator—enhanced coherence and predictability, efficiency and effectiveness of the insolvency proceedings, maximisation of chances for the debtor's recovery.

Because of the significant divergences existing between the Member State's legislations as regards the standing to bring avoidance actions, the range of legal acts that can be challenged, the duration of the suspect period, the time-limits that must be respected for the introduction of the action, the burden of proof, the available defences or the sanctions for the detrimental acts (nullity, unenforceability, compensations), the solution for the conflict of laws is a major issue. In the following, the study attempts to delineate as clearly as possible the legal regime of these actions in cross-border context. The emphasis of the difficulties or the inconveniences raised by the existing solutions will be followed by a short reflection on the possible remedies that might be implemented in the future in this field.

4.2 Nuances and Derogations to the Application of the *Lex Concursus*

4.2.1 Lex Concursus Secundarii

As a compromise between the universality and territoriality principles in cross-border insolvency proceedings, the Insolvency Regulation allows the main insolvency proceedings to be followed by one or several secondary proceedings. These will be opened in other Member State(s) than the one of the debtor's COMI[15] and their effects will be limited to the assets of the debtor situated within the territory of those Member States. The application of the Article 7(2)(m) EIR Recast in this specific context must be nuanced, as it leads to the application of a different *forum*'s *lex concursus*. In fact, upon the opening of a secondary insolvency proceedings in the State where the debtor has an establishment, the main role in the

---

[14] Virgos-Schmit Report, para 135. Since the Insolvency Regulation replaced the substance of the Convention, the guidance offered in the Report is helpful in the interpretation of the Regulation; the Report is often referred to by the Advocates General, by the European Court of Justice or by the legal scholars.

[15] Article 3(2) EIR Recast.

process of avoidance of detrimental transactions (in these proceedings) will undoubtedly be played by the *lex concursus secundarii*.[16] The reimbursements or the restitutions occurred after the admission of the corresponding avoidance actions will reintegrate the part of the estate of the debtor falling within the scope of secondary proceedings and will eventually be used for the satisfaction of the creditors who lodged their claims in these proceedings.[17]

The provisions on the avoidance of detrimental acts of the Member State's *secondary forum* may be more flexible or more liberal than those of the State of the debtor's centre of main interests. Because of this, a transaction that is unchallengeable on the basis of the legislation of the Member State of the opening of the main insolvency proceedings might be nevertheless invalidated through the application of the law governing the secondary proceedings (*lex concursus secundarii*). Even if the insolvency practitioner of the main proceedings will not be any longer entitled to act on behalf of the debtor's estate falling within the scope of the effects of the secondary proceedings (because all the corresponding powers will belong to the insolvency practitioner appointed in these secondary proceedings),[18] the differences that may exist between the different governing laws could be exploited in practice, encouraging the requests for opening secondary insolvency proceedings.[19] From this point of view, the Regulation supports at least in part the *forum shopping*; even more, it is also likely to affect the legitimate expectations of third parties that have contracted with the debtor.

Even if the limitation of the *forum shopping* was one of the main concerns during the recast process, the aspect in discussion was not specially addressed by the European legislator. The fact that under the EIR Recast the secondary proceedings may also be reorganisation proceedings, and not only winding up proceedings (as under the EIR), has no positive effect in this regard. On the contrary, it may support the requests for opening of such proceedings. Even more, the *forum shopping* might also be facilitated by the new and broader definition of the

---

[16] See Article 35 EIR Recast, former Article 28 EIR. See Fletcher, in Moss et al. 2009, p. 59, para 4.09.

[17] Even if the insolvency practitioner of the main insolvency proceedings may lodge in the secondary proceedings all the claims already lodged in the main insolvency proceedings, their rank will be determined by the *lex concursus secundarii* and with this, the general situation of creditors risks to be distorted.

[18] See Article 21(2) EIR Recast, expressly stating that the insolvency practitioner of the secondary proceedings may '*also bring any action to set aside which is in the interests of the creditors*'; after the ECJ decision in *Nortel* case, it became clear that this rule has to be followed only in so far as those actions relate to the debtor's assets that are (or were) situated within the territory of that State (see ECJ 11 June 2015—Case C-649/13). See also Virgos Schmit Report, para 91: '*In the case of secondary proceedings, the local rules on invalidation of a detrimental act shall be applicable only insofar as damage has been caused to the debtor's assets which are in this State (e.g. to the estate of the secondary proceedings). For instance, the act in question (sale, establishment of a right in rem) involves an asset which was located in this State at the relevant time*'.

[19] Alexander 2009, pp. 15–16.

establishment (as criteria of jurisdiction),[20] clearly permitting the opening of secondary proceedings also in places where the debtor has carried out non-transitory economic activity in the three-month period prior to the request to open main insolvency proceedings. The rules regarding the virtual insolvency proceedings, newly consecrated in Article 36 EIR Recast, are also of very limited help as regards the limitation of an eventual *forum shopping*. Undoubtfully, if the insolvency practitioner in the main insolvency proceedings gives an unilateral undertaking to the local creditors, the opening of secondary proceedings might be avoided and the *lex concursus secundarii* will be respected only as regards the distribution of proceeds from the realization of the corresponding assets and the priority rights of local creditors. But if the insolvency practitioner wants to open secondary proceedings precisely in order to benefit from a more favourable law regarding the avoidance of detrimental transaction (the *lex concursus secundarii*), it is highly improbable that he will give such an undertaking.

4.2.2   Derogations to the Lex Fori Concursus *in Favour of* Lex Situs, Lex Laboris, Lex Registry *or* Lex Mercatus

The application of the *lex fori concursus* is subject to some express derogations, attesting once again the compromise made by the European legislator confronted with the disparities among the Member States' legislations in the field of insolvency. Thus, in accordance with Article 11 EIR Recast, the effects of insolvency proceedings on a contract conferring the right to acquire or make use of immovable property are governed solely by the law of the Member State in whose territory the immovable property is situated. The effects of insolvency proceedings on employment contracts shall be determined solely by the law of the Member State applicable to the contract of employment (Article 13 EIR Recast). In accordance with Article 14 EIR Recast, the effects of insolvency proceedings on the rights of a debtor in immovable property, a ship or an aircraft subject to registration in a public register are governed by the law of the Member State under whose authority the register is kept. Finally, Article 12 EIR Recast provides that the effects of insolvency proceedings on the rights and obligations of participants to a payment or settlement system or to a financial market are governed solely by the law of the Member State applicable to that system or market; the second paragraph confirms the application of the law of the same State for the potential actions for voidness, voidability or unenforceability which may be taken to set aside payments or transactions concluded by such parties.

---

[20] Designed to protect the interests of local creditors in a jurisdiction where the debtor is no longer active at the moment of the request to open main insolvency proceedings, this new definition, found in Article 2(10) EIR Recast, is broader than the one previously set out in Article 2(h) EIR.

In the EIR Recast, these solutions were kept unchanged. The important concessions made to the application of *lex concursus* are dictated by the disparities among the Members States' legislations and they reflect the political choice of the European legislator to protect some categories of creditors from the unexpected interference of a foreign (possibly unknown) insolvency law, to protect trade and to maintain the legal certainty. The universal reach of *lex concursus* is undermined, but as long as no harmonisation was made at the level of substantial law, a different solution was difficult to achieve.

4.2.3 The Lex Causae—'Veto' to the Application of Lex Fori Concursus

The most important exception to the application of *lex fori concursus* is provided by Article 16 EIR Recast (former Article 13 EIR), a text which represents an attempt of the European legislator to ensure a proper balance between, on the one hand, the interests of third parties who have concluded with the (now insolvent) debtor some acts or operations perfectly valid under the *lex causae* and, on the other hand, the protection of the general body of creditors, who may challenge the effectiveness of those acts on the basis of the *lex fori concursus*. The avoidance permitted by *lex concursus* will be blocked when the act is subject to the law of a Member State other than the State of the opening of proceedings and that law does not allow any means of challenging it in the relevant case.

4.2.3.1 Justification

According to Recital 67 from the Preamble, the rule is inspired by the need to respect the legitimate interests of the third parties who could reasonably rely, as regards the validity and effectiveness of the contracts concluded with the debtor, on the provisions of the particular law governing those contracts (from the moment of their conclusion).[21] The need to protect the legitimate interests of the third parties is all the more intense in cases in which the determination of the debtor's centre of main interests (and of the *lex concursus*) is not very obvious and also when, following a transfer of its COMI to another Member State, the debtor circumvented the law governing both the insolvency proceedings and the eventual avoidance actions,[22] with a surprising (and possible detrimental) effect for its foreign business

---

[21] On the willingness of the European legislator to support within the Member States' territories the confidence in the efficacy of acts governed on the merits by a law different than the *lex concursus*—see Virgos-Schmit Report, para 136. Moss and Smith in Moss et al. 2009, p. 297, para 8.231; Pfeiffer 2013, pp. 310–311; Linna 2014, p. 82.

[22] On the *forum shopping* in cross-border insolvency proceedings, see McCormack 2009, pp. 169 et seq; Eidenmuller 2009, pp. 1–28.

partners. The recognition of the possibility for those persons to rely, when defending the validity and effects of a legal act concluded with the debtor, on the law governing that act—a law firmly determined or determinable from the very moment of its conclusion—strengthens the legal certainty and stability and corresponds to the expectations of those persons. Even if in the EIR Recast the European legislator intervened in order to limit the impact that a deliberate and potential abusive modification of the debtor's COMI may have on the insolvency proceedings, the concerns presented above are still justified[23] and this may explain why the role of *lex causae* was kept unchanged in the EIR Recast.

This emphasis on the legitimate interests implies that contracts in respect of which Article 16 EIR Recast can be invoked should be concluded prior to the opening of the insolvency proceedings. For contracts concluded or acts performed after this moment, any expectations of the third parties in the effectiveness of that contract or act beyond or despite the *lex concursus* provisions are no longer justified.[24]

The protection of third parties on the basis of *lex causae* may also have strong negative effects on the insolvency estate and on the collective interests of the creditors, because the dismissal of the avoidance action will limit both the possibilities for the reconstruction and maximisation of the insolvency estate and the chances for the business' rescue or for bigger distributions to creditors. For this reason and also because when contracting with a foreign debtor, the counterparty assumes the (predictable) risk that the *lex concursus* of the foreign State may intervene to affect the effectiveness of that contract, some legal scholars challenged the opportunity of the mere presence of Article 13 EIR.[25] In the Recast, the

---

[23] In fact, the efficacy of the transfer of social (registered and/or real) seat of a company within EU is generally supported and reinforced at the EU level (see ECJ 16.12.2008—Case C-210/06 (*Cartesio*); ECJ 12.07.2012—Case C-378/10 (*VALE Epitesi*); ECJ 25.10.2017—Case C-106/16 (*Polbud*); see also the Proposal for a Directive of the European Parliament and of the Council amending Directive (EU) 2017/1132 as regards cross-border conversions, mergers and divisions, COM(2018)241). This is a business decision for which the debtor has a large freedom, according to its economic and legal interest. Even if it may imply also a change of the (future) applicable insolvency law, the debtor's current contractual partners do not (yet) have the power to prevent such a change, which might adversely affect their interests.

[24] See *mutatis mutandis*, ECJ 16.1.2014—Case C-328/12 (*R. Schmid*) para 35. See also ECJ 15.10.2015—Case C-557/13 (*Lutz*) para 35: '*As from the opening of insolvency proceedings, the creditors of the debtor concerned are able to predict the effects of the application of the lex fori concursus on the legal relations which they maintain with that debtor [and...] they cannot therefore in principle claim to benefit from greater protection*'.

[25] See for example Veder 2011, p. 86, which proposed the simple repeal of the Article 13 of the Regulation 1346/2000. Also, Bureau 2002, pp. 640–641, para 41; Bogdan, in Moss et al. 2009, p. 297, para 8.233; Kolmann 2011, p. 9. This position can be easily sustained. Normally, the applicability of the insolvency law of a certain legal system is determined on the basis of objective connecting factors (like COMI, in the EU Member States), designed to prevent frauds and to ensure proper protection for the public interests at stake on the forum State. There cannot be legitimate expectations in the intervention of the *insolvency provisions* of a *lex causae* sometimes freely designated by the parties. Eventually, some legitimate expectations may exist as regards the

European legislator was not prepared to make this step and, as in the EIR, it favoured the protection of interests of some creditors to the collective interest of all creditors and to the unitary treatment of all detrimental acts. To measure the importance of this solution, some precisions are necessary on the functioning of Article 16 (as described by the legal scholars or imposed by the ECJ's case law).

4.2.3.2 Functioning

Article 16 EIR Recast represents an effective way of defence for the third parties confronted with an avoidance action. The *lex concursus* will be ignored and the act will maintain its effects, its validity and efficacy, when the interested person succeeds to prove that the act is governed by the law of a Member State other than the State of the opening of proceedings, when this law does not allow under any circumstance its invalidation. The *lex causae* is generally known by the parties from the conclusion of the act (unlike *lex concursus*, dependent of the localisation of the debtor's COMI or establishment on the territory of a certain Member State, in a future moment) and will have the last word regarding the avoidance. In other words, an avoidance action admissible under *lex concursus* will succeed only if the act would be also challengeable according to *lex causae*.[26]

Lex causae will have a role to play only to determine whether the act can be challenged or not. Thus, when it allows means of challenging the act in the relevant case, the defence provided by Article 16 will be neutralized and the regime of the avoidance action will be entirely established by the *lex concursus* (as provided in Article 7(2)(m) EIR Recast). This solution is welcomed: the intervention of two laws is required only as regards the admissibility of *actio pauliana*. If the *pauliana* is admissible, its regime and consequences are established on the basis of only one law (*lex concursus*) and the possible difficulties of adaptation are avoided.

---

intervention of those provisions of the *lex causae* applicable to the (individual) avoidance actions in the absence of insolvency proceedings (such as Article 2901 Italian Civil Code, Articles 3:45 to 3:48 Dutch Civil Code, Articles 1111 and 1291.3 Spanish Civil Code, Article 1341.2 French Civil Code). But, as it will be explained *infra* (para 3.2.4), on the basis of the indications from Virgos-Schmit Report (para 136), the case law does not make today such a distinction.

[26] The determination of the *lex causae* may sometimes raise problems. Normally, when the detrimental act whose avoidance is requested in the context of insolvency proceedings is a contract, the determination of the applicable law—*lex causae*—will be done in accordance with the *Rome I* Regulation or with the legal instruments which preceded it in time in the forum State. If the detrimental act is a security interest in a collateral, the *lex rei sitae* will intervene in order to solve the problem of enforceability of that security interest in respect of third parties—see Dammann and Pigot 2016, p. 529. Given the difficulties of identification of the *lex causae* and the inconveniences raised by the existing solution, some authors proposed to interpret the 'safe harbour rule' from Article 13 EIR as a rule referring to the law with the closest connection to, or the greatest interest of defining the voidability of, the act in question—see Alexander 2009, pp. 19 et seq. In the EIR Recast, the EU legislator did not take position on this aspect.

Article 16 EIR Recast provides an exception to the *lex concursus'* competence and it must be interpreted restrictively. It will not be applied *ex officio* by courts and *lex concursus* will be disregarded only at the request of the third party opposing the avoidance action, who must prove that, according to a foreign law, the operation is unchallengeable in the given circumstances of the case.[27] This involves both the proof of the content of the foreign law (*lex causae*) and of the factual aspects, objective or subjective, positive or negative, pertinent for its protection.[28] These aspects were detailed by the ECJ in its case law and they will be explained infra.

A question may arise as to the possibility of displacement of the *lex concursus* when the *lex causae* does not permit the avoidance of the act, but obliges the third party to pay compensation for the value of the transaction. Some legal scholars already alleged that the solution should be searched not in the letter, but in the spirit of Article 16 EIR Recast. Because the relevant issue is not necessarily the formal upholding of the act, but the actual patrimonial gain for the third party (which is lost, if the *lex causae* impose such a compensation), they considered that the defence provided (by the former Article 13 EIR) should not operate in the hypothesis under discussion.[29] A possible supporting argument for this (broad) position might also be extracted from the *Kornhaas* judgment, in which ECJ stated that a national law obliging the manager director to reimburse to the company the payments made before the opening of the insolvency proceedings but after the company had become insolvent '*appears at least similar to a rule laying down the 'unenforceability of legal acts detrimental to all the creditors*'.[30] This last judgment raises nevertheless some doubts and new discussions, since it is not clear if the acts covered by rules 'at least similar' to those regarding the avoidance could benefit from the Article 16 EIR Recast.

In September 2017 a new request for a preliminary ruling was lodged to the ECJ[31] and one of the questions referred regards precisely the operation of the (now) Article 16 EIR Recast in case of actions for recovery of damages based on the wrongful behaviour of that third party towards the creditors. On 18 October 2018 the Advocate general Bobek delivered its opinion. After expressing doubts about the applicability of EIR (Recast) in the matter, he considered that this action cannot be qualified as a rule 'relating to the voidness, voidability or unenforceability of legal acts detrimental to all the creditors' and, consequently, the third

---

[27] See the Virgos-Schmit Report, para 136. The solution can easily be justified if one takes into account the purpose of the text: to save the legitimate expectations of third parties regarding the validity of an act (according to the law which governs it), against the surprising interference of the *lex concursus*.

[28] See Linna 2015, p. 577.

[29] See Linna 2014, pp. 84–85: '*The heart of the protection is that the third party can rely on the fact that he has the right to keep the value of the transaction, not that the transaction itself is guaranteed*'.

[30] ECJ 10.12.2015—Case C-594/14 (*Kornhaas*).

[31] Case C-535/17 (*NK, liquidator in the bankruptcies of OJ B.V. and PI v BNP Paribas Fortis N.V.*).

party cannot rely on the exception in Article 16 EIR Recast.[32] The wording of the provision (referring to the *person who benefited* from an act detrimental to the creditors) and its purpose (the protection of the *legitimate expectations* of a person who has benefited from an act detrimental to all the creditors) supports this position and precludes the applicability of Article 16 EIR Recast in case of actions for damages brought by a liquidator against a third party having acted wrongfully towards the creditors. In its judgment,[33] the ECJ took the simpler path and held that, since it was based on the ordinary rules of civil and commercial law, the tortious action was not in fact governed by the Insolvency Regulation, but by Brussels I Recast.[34] This answer left without object the preliminary questions regarding the applicable law and the possible intervention of Article 16 EIR Recast. Nevertheless, given the characterisation retained, it become clear that the merits of the claim will be governed not by the choice of law rules from the EIR Recast, but by the general choice of law rules for non-contractual obligations (forum State's rules or Rome II Regulation).

4.2.3.3   Limitations

The intervention of Article 16 EIR Recast is limited in two ways, proving once again the complexity of the system created by the European legislator.

On the one hand, the *lex concursus* could only be disregarded if the foreign *lex causae* belongs to another EU Member State. If the transaction is governed by the law of a non-EU Member State, Article 16 will not intervene and the avoidance action will be exclusively governed by the law of the EU Member State of the opening of the proceedings. This limitation might be justified by the legislator's intention to prevent the purposive designation as *lex contractus* of a law of a State not admitting the *pauliana* at all or admitting it in extremely restrictive conditions, quasi-impossible to be met. The introduction of Article 13 EIR, now Article 16, was only a compromise designed to protect the third parties. The fact that all the Member States' legislations consecrated the possibility of avoidance actions, even if in different ways and with different limits, was probably seemed as the minimum counterbalance offered for the protection of the general body of the creditors and of the insolvency estate. Nevertheless, the solution found in Article 16 EIR Recast stands in contrast with the broad admission of the jurisdiction of the Member

---

[32] Opinion of AG Bobek, at para 94–96.

[33] ECJ 6.02.2019—Case C-535/17 (*NK*).

[34] The links with the insolvency proceedings—action brought by the liquidator in the interest of all creditors, with proceeds that fall into the bankrupt estate—were held irrelevant, as they regard only the procedural context of the claim that do not derive directly from insolvency law (paras 32–33 from the judgment). The accent was on the fact that the legal basis of the action was not found in derogating rules specific to insolvency proceedings, as required by the previous ECJ's case law (4.09.2014—Case C-157/13, *Nickel & Goeldner Spedition*) and nowadays by the Article 6 EIR Recast (paras 26–27).

States' courts to decide actions to set transactions aside brought against defendants domiciled in non-EU States[35] (and the correlative application of the *lex fori concursus*), and for this reason it is also vulnerable to criticism.[36]

On the other hand, Article 16 EIR Recast will not operate when the avoidance action concerns a contract conferring the right to acquire or make use of immoveable property (Article 11), a contract concluded between parties to a payment or settlement system or to a financial market (Article 12), an employment contract or its performance (Article 13), a right in immovable property, a ship or an aircraft subject to registration in a public register (Article 14).[37] In such cases, the special conflict of laws rules established for each of these categories of contracts prevail over the rule from Article 7 of the Regulation and its corrective from Article 16. The laws designated by the former will have priority as well and will enjoy exclusivity, including as regards the avoidance actions,[38] whatever the *lex concursus* may be. These rules, some inspired also by protection aims,[39] are enabling the contracting parties to base their expectations upon a single set of rules, regardless the insolvency law that may happen to govern one of them. Thus, legal certainty is strengthened. But the tasks of the insolvency practitioner will not be easy and will imply supplementary costs, since he must identify,[40] inform about and comply with the relevant provisions of the insolvency law of the Member State governing each of the transactions he wants to set aside.

A (further) important factor of complication must nevertheless be considered: the special conflict of laws rules from Articles 11, 12, 13 and 14 will apply only insofar

---

[35] See ECJ 16.1.2014—Case C-328/12 (*R. Schmid*).

[36] Linna 2015, p. 575.

[37] A different solution exists as regards the special rules provided in Articles 8, 9 and 10 EIR Recast. At a first sight, Articles 8(4), 9(2) and 10(3) refer only to Article 7(2)(m) EIR Recast, which will entail to the sole application of the *lex concursus* for the avoidance actions of the rights *in rem*, of the contracts that generate obligations for which a set-off will be demanded in the proceedings or of the contracts which provide an eventual reservation of title. Such an interpretation is not correct: Article 7(2)(m) realizes a particularisation of Article 7(1) and should be read in connection with it; any reference to Article 7(2)(m) should be understood also to this text. Since Article 7(1) provides for the application of the *lex concursus* '*save as otherwise provided in this Regulation*', Article 16 will have a role to play in regards of such actions. This position is confirmed by the European case law on Article 13 EIR: see ECJ 15.10.2015—Case C-557/13 (*Lutz*), which will be detailed *infra*.

[38] The solution is express in Article 12(2) EIR Recast and can be easily deduced from the broad formulation of Articles 11 and 13.

[39] See Recitals 71 and 72 from the Preamble.

[40] If *lex rei sitae* or *lex mercatus* are not raising important challenges from this point of view, the situation is different as regards the law governing the employment contracts. The solutions found in Article 8 of the Rome I Regulation and in the corresponding case law of the ECJ are rather complex. Difficulties may arise, for example, as regards the articulation of *lex voluntatis* and *lexi loci laboris*, the identification of *lex loci laboris*, the role of the escape clause, the intervention of some internationally mandatory rules and, because of this, the determination of the applicable law becomes sometimes certain only after the intervention of a court—see Moreno in Magnus and Mankowski 2017, pp. 586 et seq.

as they designate the law of a Member State. When this condition is not met, a return to the general rules should be followed and a discussion is possible precisely as regards the identification of those general rules.

Following the Virgos-Schmidt Report,[41] important authors consider that the norms to be taken into account are the particular private international law rules provided by the forum State for these situations.[42] In our opinion, this solution could be discussed in the light of the recent developments in the ECJ's case law. The Regulation has unified the choice of law rules for cross-border insolvencies and when it is applicable (when the debtor's COMI is located within the European Union), the newly stipulated rules—including choice of law rules—replace all the previous norms existing in the Members States' legislations.[43] According to the Court of Justice's position in the *Schmid* case, the texts of the Regulation do not support the conclusion that the existing jurisdiction rules should not apply when the debtor has assets located outside the EU or is involved in contracts performed outside of the EU.[44] On the contrary, some of the Recitals from the Preamble, detailing the

---

[41] Virgos-Schmit Report, para 44(b): '*Even when the centre of a debtor's main interests is in a Contracting State and the Convention is applicable, its provisions are restricted to relations with other Contracting States. Where non-Member States are concerned, it is the responsibility of each Member State to define the appropriate conflict rules. Hence, for example, Article 8 governs the effects of insolvency proceedings on contracts relating to the immovable property of the debtor, as an exception to the general applicability of the law of the State of the opening (ex Article 4), but is applicable only when the immovable property is located in a Contracting State. If the asset in question is situated in a non-Contracting State, the Convention does not govern the case. It is for the State opening the proceedings to decide whether or not an exception to the general applicability of its law is advisable, and under what terms*'. Even clearer are the provisions of para 93: '*The exceptions to the application of the law of the State of the opening (Article 4) are referred to in Articles 5 to 15 of the Convention. Apart from Articles 6 and 14, which by systemic arguments must be interpreted in the same way, the exception is made in favour of the law of a 'Contracting State'. This does not mean that, by a contrario interpretation, the law of the State of the opening of proceedings is applicable where the State concerned is not a Contracting State. The need to protect legitimate expectations and the certainty of transactions is equally valid in relations with non-Contracting States. The group's intention was simply to regulate these cases in line with the general restriction of the Convention to the intra-Community effect of insolvency proceedings (see point 44). Contracting States are, therefore, free to decide which rules they deem most appropriate in other cases (the same ones as in Articles 5 to 15 of the Convention, or others)*'.

[42] See Fletcher, in Moss et al. 2009, p. 70, para 4.31 and p. 71, para 4.33.

[43] Recital 66 from the Preamble.

[44] ECJ 16.1.2014—Case C-328/12 (*R. Schmid*) para 25: '*it is apparent, however, from recital 4 that that objective makes it necessary, in particular, 'to avoid incentives for the parties to transfer assets or judicial proceedings from one Member State to another, seeking to obtain a more favourable legal position (forum shopping)'. Recital 8 refers to the objective of 'improving the efficiency and effectiveness of insolvency proceedings having cross-border effects' and recital 12 states that insolvency proceedings falling within the Regulation's field of application 'have universal scope and aim at encompassing all the debtor's assets'. The latter objectives may encompass not solely relations between Member States but, by their nature and in accordance with their wording, any cross-border situation*'. Even if this solution is contrary to the original ideas of the European legislator, it was not changed during the reform from 2015. Given the simplification operated, it was considered opportune by some authors—see Jault Seseke and

aims of the text, militate for a broader interpretation of the Regulation's scope.[45]
Even if *Schmid* concerned a matter of jurisdiction, the Court made clear that the
Regulation can be applied also to non-purely European insolvency proceedings and
the arguments advanced may also operate, *mutatis mutandis*, as regard choice of law
issues.[46] Consequently, since Articles 11–13 EIR Recast are mere exceptions to the
basic rule from Article 7, it follows that when the specific requirements for their
application are not met, the primary rule dictating the application of the substantial
and procedural provisions of the *lex concursus* and also its general corrective from
Article 16 should come into play. As mentioned, the issue is nevertheless contro-
versial and the ECJ's guidance on this point would be necessary. The divergences
between the Member States' legislations are important and the uncertainty in this
field impedes on the uniform application of the Regulation and may have negative
effects on the interested parties. From this point of view, the fact that the EU legislator
did not addressed the issue in the recast process might be seen as a lost opportunity to
bring more clarity in the functioning of the Regulation.

4.3   The Perpetuation of the Inconveniences Raised by the Texts in Spite of the ECJ's Guidance

In its recent case law, the Court of Justice has already provided on three occasions
some guidance on the interpretation of Article 13 EIR, predecessor of Article 16
EIR Recast. This proves that the complexity of the texts is doubled by important
practical complications, which contradicts the objectives of efficacy, coherence and
legal certainty for cross-border insolvency proceedings, followed by the European
legislator.

Robine 2014, p. 917. See also ECJ 11.06.2015—Case C-649/13 (*Nortel*) para 49: '*It should also
be noted that it is apparent from recitals 6 and 23 in the preamble to Regulation No 1346/2000,
first, that that regulation sets out uniform rules on conflict of laws which replace national rules of
private international law and, second, that that replacement is limited, in accordance with the
principle of proportionality, to the field of application of the rules laid down by that regulation.
Thus, the regulation does not preclude, in principle, all application, in the context of a related
action, such as those before the referring court, of the legislation of the Member State of the court
before which that action is pending, relating to the private international law of that State, in so far
as Regulation No 1346/2000 does not contain a uniform rule governing the situation at issue*'.

[45] See Recitals 3, 4, 8, 23, 25 from the Preamble.

[46] See nevertheless Dammann and Bleicher 2014, p. 1710. These authors consider that the harmonisation of the Member States' private international law rules regarding the jurisdiction for
insolvency related actions and the simplification operated is the most interesting effect of this
judgment (p. 1710), but refuse its broad application, beyond aspects similar to the case in hands.
They remain vague on the issue of applicability of the general choice of law rule from the
Regulation and concentrate mostly on the extension of the principle of the universality of the main
insolvency proceedings outside the territory of the European Union, an outcome considered
desirable, but also hampered by the absence of the automatic recognition of (insolvency) judgments outside the EU (p. 1713).

4.3.1 Lutz *Judgment*

The first pertinent judgment on the matter, *Lutz*,[47] was pronounced in April 2015 in a case in which the German BGH requested clarifications on the interpretation of now Articles 7(2)(m) and 16 EIR Recast and on the delimitation of the corresponding scopes of *lex concursus* and *lex causae*.

4.3.1.1 Nuances Regarding the Category of Acts in Favour of Which Article 16 May Be Invoked

The first issue brought before the ECJ regarded the delimitation of the category of acts in favour of which Article 16 EIR Recast may be invoked (*in casu*, the challenged payment was made after the opening of insolvency proceedings, but on the basis of a right to attach that was established before the opening of those proceedings). The general rules of interpretation already formulated in the doctrine were of course followed. The Court recalled that Article 16 provides for an exception to the general rule of application of the *lex fori concursus* and, as a consequence, it should be interpreted in a strict manner and proportionate to the objective pursued—the protection of the legitimate expectations of third parties and of the legal certainty of transactions in Member States other than that of the opening of the proceedings.[48] Taking into account the fact that from the moment of the opening of the proceedings, the creditors may easily foresee the effects of the application of the *lex fori concursus* on the legal relationships they have with the debtor,[49] the Court stated without big surprise that Article 16 '*is not, in principle, applicable to acts which take place after the opening of insolvency proceedings*'.[50]

A nuance in this position was nevertheless possible, because *in casu* the creditor had obtained the attachment of the debtor's accounts before the opening of the insolvency proceedings. Considering that the corresponding right (the right to

---

[47] ECJ 15.10.2015—Case C-557/13 (*Lutz*); Vallens 2015, p. 755. In this case, Mr. Lutz, an Austrian purchaser of a car never delivered to him, obtained in Austria an enforceable payment order against the debtor, ECZ Austria, the Austrian subsidiary of a German company. After the debtor's application for the opening of main insolvency proceedings in Germany, but prior to the court judgment on the opening, Mr. Lutz obtained from the Austrian courts a leave to enforce that order and three Austrian bank accounts of the debtor were attached. The sums were afterwards paid, and the insolvency practitioner brought an action in front of German courts to set aside the payment, action perfectly admissible according to the German law, *lex concursus*. Both in first instance and on appeal, Mr. Lutz tried unsuccessfully to obtain a dismissal on the basis of the Austrian law, which considered the action as time-barred, since it was not introduced within one year after the opening of the proceedings. The BGH, finally seised with the case, decided to refer three preliminary questions to the European Court of Justice.

[48] ECJ, *Lutz*, paras 34–35.

[49] A similar solution was consecrated before, as regards the jurisdiction—see ECJ 16.1.2014—Case C-328/12 (*R. Schmid*) para 35.

[50] ECJ, *Lutz*, para 36.

attach the credit balance on the debtor company's bank accounts) may be a right *in rem*, for which the European legislator provided a special protection—the recognition of possibility for their proprietor to enforce it over the collateral, through a segregation or a separate settlement of the security in spite of the debtor's insolvency (Article 5 EIR, now Article 8 EIR Recast)—the Court made a distinction, justified by the need to ensure the *effet utile* of that Article. The allegation according to which Article 16 EIR Recast is not, in principle, applicable to acts that occurred after the opening of the insolvency proceedings cannot be transposed to the acts by which the creditor enforced a right *in rem* (valid according to the *lex situs*), falling within the scope of Article 8(1) EIR Recast. The need to ensure the effectiveness of Article 8(1) requires, on the contrary, that, when confronted with an action challenging the validity of acts of enforcement of a right *in rem*, carried out after the opening of the insolvency proceedings, the secured creditor should be able to rely on Article 16 and on the law governing that act—a law of a Member State other than that of the opening of the proceedings—to block the avoidance action.[51]

In our opinion, the weakness of this reasoning is related to the fact that the enforcement in cross-border insolvency proceedings, in different forms, of a right *in rem* validly created according to *lex situs*, emanates directly from the Regulation and not from the *lex causae* (*lex rei situs*). In the case under scrutiny, the insolvency practitioner challenged both the attachment of the debtor's banking account (the valid creation of the right *in rem*) and the payment made on the basis of this attachment after the opening of the proceedings. The ECJ did not discuss the right *in rem* (whose validity was supposed to be acquired), but only the payment.[52] Because the payment is nothing more than the enforcement/the realisation of the right *in rem*, it should have been validated by the Court directly on the basis of Article 8 EIR Recast, without considering the provisions of *lex concursus* or of *lex causae* (*lex rei sitae*). Or, at least this is how the authors are currently interpreting the expression '*The opening of insolvency proceedings shall not affect the rights in rem of creditors or third parties...*'.[53] The Court did not follow this path, but imposed a more complex approach, doubling somehow the requirements of the legal text. In fact, it actually considered that the right *in rem* validly acquired will not be affected by the opening of the insolvency proceedings only if (neither) the

---

[51] ECJ, *Lutz*, paras 41–42.

[52] It is doubtful that its conclusions would have been the same if it would have approached the issue from the point of view of the creation of the right. In fact, one of the common fraudulent transactions are those through which a security interest is created over the debtor's estate or assets. In our opinion, the possibility to invoke a foreign *lex causae* (*lex situs*) according to Article 16 EIR Recast for the security interests created after the opening of the insolvency proceedings would be an open invitation to circumvent the *lex concursus* provisions. Because of this, the paras 41–49 of the decision should be read with precaution: as regards the acts intervened after the opening of the insolvency proceedings, Article 16 can be invoked only if their object was *the exercise* or *the enforcement* of rights *in rem*.

[53] Bureau 2002, p. 660, para 76; Menjucq 2005, pp. 48–49; Fletcher, in Moss et al. 2009, p. 61, para 4.12.

insolvency provisions of the *lex situs* do not permit such a challenge.[54] Once more, the problem is generated by the way in which the Court is approaching the case. As regards the validity of the creation of the right *in rem*, the conflict between *lex concursus* and *lex causae* (*lex rei sitae*) is allowed by the Regulation (Article 8(4) EIR Recast), and thus Article 16 would have a role to play. Instead, as regards the exercise of a right *in rem* validly created, Article 8(1) EIR Recast suppresses the conflict between *lex concursus* and *lex causae* and imposes a substantive rule authorising directly the realisation of this right, in spite of the insolvency proceedings opened in another Member State than that of the *situs*. The ECJ disregarded the distinction between the two hypotheses, preferring a different interpretation for Article 8(1) EIR Recast. Thus, it was conducted to discuss the other preliminary questions referred to it by the BGH.

4.3.1.2 The Broad Scope of the *Lex Causae*

The delimitation of the specific scopes of the *lex concursus* (providing for a three-year limitation period for bringing an action to set aside a transaction) and of the *lex causae* (providing for a shorter limitation period, one year from the opening of the insolvency proceedings, not respected *in casu*) was the second important issue discussed. Emphasising that Article 16 EIR Recast does not make any distinction between the substantive and the procedural provisions of the *lex causae*, while the exclusion of procedural provisions from the scope of that article would lead to arbitrary discriminations according to the legal-theory models adopted by the Member States and would undermine the much needed uniformity in the application of the Regulation,[55] the Court stated that the *lex causae* can be taken into account for both the principle of the admission of the action to set aside transactions and as well as for its modalities, and in particular for the limitation periods or other time-bars relating to this action.

Although in the first part of the judgment, the Court mentioned the need for a strict interpretation of Article 16 EIR Recast, it actually gave preference to the need to protect the legitimate expectations of the parties involved and the certainty of transactions, reserving a quite broad scope of application for the *lex causae*. Its intervention is contemplated not only for substantive but also for procedural defences, a seemingly acceptable solution if the practical difficulties related to the characterisation are taken into account. Nevertheless, the risk for a cumulative application of the competing laws (*lex concursus* and *lex causae*, its insolvency

---

[54] This perspective is similar to that imposed by Articles 11–14 EIR Recast, even if the differences of formulation (and effects) of these texts are evident.

[55] See paras 46–48 and 55. The Court refuses the application of Rome I Regulation as regards the limitation periods for the actions to set transactions aside falling within the scope of Articles 4 and 13 EIR (para 46). Its solution is nevertheless consistent with the one provided by Article 12(1)(d) Rome I, which provides the application of *lex contractus* to the various ways of extinguishing obligations, like prescription and other ways of time-bar.

provisions included) is a high one. For the insolvency practitioner, the obligation to comply with the standards of two different laws for each transaction that he purports to set aside will harden his mission, while its chances for success will be undermined.[56]

4.3.2 Nike *Judgment*

The second judgment relevant for the understanding of the Article 16 EIR Recast was pronounced also in 2015, in the *Nike* case,[57] in which the referring court—Court of Appeal of Helsinki—was confronted with difficulties of interpretation of the expression "*does not allow any means of challenging that act in the relevant case*", doubled by uncertainties regarding the burden of proof and the obligations of the third party relying on *lex causae* to adduce evidence on the content of that law.

4.3.2.1 Application *in Concreto* of the *Lex Causae*

Recalling the indication given in the *Lutz* case on the restrictive interpretation of Article 16 EIR Recast, the ECJ stated that it would be inadequate to take into consideration the *lex causae* only when, on the basis of its provisions, the act at issue would have, in a purely abstract manner, an unchallengeable character. On the contrary, the need to protect the legitimate expectations of the persons who have benefited from that act and the certainty of transactions within the European Union would require that all the circumstances of the case be considered. This solution

---

[56] See also Fritz 2011, p. 14: '*the avoidance regime which least favours avoidance action takes precedence over the more generous regime from the point of view of the creditor*'.

[57] ECJ 15.10.2015—Case C-310/14 (*Nike European Operations Netherlands*); Dammann and Pigot 2016, p. 525. The case concerned the insolvency proceedings in respect of Sportland, a Finnish company that, in the months prior to the opening, paid some outstanding debts to its franchisor, the Dutch company Nike. In the insolvency proceedings conducted according to the Finnish law, Sportland brought an action for annulment of the payments (*Finnish Law on recovery of assets* allowed the challenge of the payments of debts made by the debtor within three months of the prescribed date, when they were paid with unusual means of payment, prematurely or in an amount considered significant in view of the value of the debtor's estate (para 6 of the judgment). Seeking the dismissal of that action, Nike relied on the substantial provisions of the Netherlands law, which allowed the avoidance only in limited conditions, not fulfilled (apparently) in the case ((1) when the recipient received the payment, he was aware that the application for insolvency proceedings had already been lodged or (2) the payment was agreed between the creditor and the debtor in order to give priority to that creditor to the detriment of the other creditors—para 7 of the judgment).

was found in the Virgos-Schmit Report[58] and is also favoured by the doctrine.[59] But as regards the interpretation of the Article 16 EIR Recast, the result is not probably that restrictive as expected. According to the Court, in order to circumvent the *lex concursus*, it is not necessary to prove that, in general, an act similar to the one in question may not be challenged on the basis of *lex causae*. On the contrary, it is sufficient for the third party seeking for protection to establish, taking into account all the particularities of the case at issue, that the avoidance action will fail under *lex causae* because, for example, it was not brought by the person having *locus standi* for it, because the general scope of the avoiding powers was not respected, because the act was not concluded in the (shorter) suspect period, because any other defences provided by that law may operate. This analysis *in concreto* of each situation increases the risks for the *lex concursus* to be overlooked by the *lex causae* and, consequently, the uncertainty for the insolvency practitioner as regards the results of the avoidance actions also becomes more important. The missions of the national courts, confronted with the possible application of two laws for each transaction challenged in a cross-border insolvency proceedings, will be hardened as well.

4.3.2.2 The Burden of Proof

The Court was further concerned with a procedural issue: to determine which party is required to plead and to bear the burden of proof as regards the (non)-compliance with the requirements provided by the *lex causae* for the voidness, voidability or unenforceability of the act. Following a literal interpretation of the text, the Court clarified without big difficulties that is for the defendant in the avoidance action, relying on the provisions of the *lex causae*, to prove both the facts from which can be drawn the conclusion that the act is unchallengeable and the absence of any evidence that would militate against that conclusion.[60] The applicant cannot be required to claim, or even prove, that the conditions for the application of a provision of the *lex causae* which, in principle, would enable the act at issue to be challenged are satisfied.[61] A simple allegation by the defendant of the unchallengeable character of that act according to the *lex causae* would not be sufficient. Such a precision is able to safeguard the key role for the *lex concursus* and, since it manages to ensure an equilibrium between the defendant (the third party who benefits from the act) and the claimant (probably, the insolvency practitioner acting for the estate), it is welcomed.

---

[58] The *Virgos-Schmit* Report states that the expression '*in the relevant case*' means that '*the act should not be capable of being challenged in fact i.e. after taking into account all the concrete circumstances of the case. It is not sufficient to determine whether it can be challenged in the abstract …*' (para 137).

[59] See Linna 2014, p. 82. Fletcher, in Moss et al. 2009, para 4.38, p. 74.

[60] ECJ, *Nike*, para 25.

[61] ECJ, *Nike*, para 26.

This autonomous solution was further detailed by the Court in her response: only after the defendant has first adduced sufficient evidence that the circumstances enabling the act to be challenged on the basis of the *lex causae* do not exist, the competent court may decide that it is for the applicant to prove the existence of a provision or principle of the *lex causae* on the basis of which the act can actually be challenged.[62]

4.3.2.3 The Articulation with the National Law

Despite these clarifications, deduced from the letter and the purpose of Article 16 EIR Recast, the national laws still have a role to play in this area. In the absence of an ample European harmonisation of the procedural norms related to the implementation of this text, the rule established by the European legislator should be completed with more detailed provisions regarding, for example, the ways in which the evidence is to be elicited, the evidence admissible in front of the competent court, the principles governing the assessment, by the competent court, of the probative value of the evidence adduced before it. These provisions will be provided by the legislation of the forum state (*lex fori*),[63] applied in accordance with the principle of procedural autonomy and its necessary correctives, the principles of equivalence and effectiveness.[64]

4.3.2.4 The Large Scope of the *Lex Causae*

Finally, the Court detailed the meaning and the limits of the reference to the *lex causae*. Insisting on the fact that the legitimate expectations of the defendant (the person who has benefited from the act detrimental to all the creditors) must be protected, it decided that the *lex causae* will include not only the special norms devoted to insolvency proceedings (as in *Lutz* judgment), but also its provisions and general principles, taken as a whole.[65] This last extension—which seemingly

---

[62] ECJ, *Nike*, para 45.

[63] ECJ, *Nike*, paras 27–28.

[64] In particular, related to the latter, the Court also gave two useful indications, that strengthen the uniform solution deduced from the letter of Article 16 EIR Recast. First, ECJ expressly ruled that is precluded the application of national procedural rules that would make excessively difficult or impossible in practice the exercise of the rights conferred by the Article 16 EIR Recast, especially in connection with proof of the negative, namely that certain circumstances did not exist. Loyal to the need to interpret strictly the legal text, the Court also clarified that the mere difficulties to prove the respect of the conditions set by the *lex causae* for the validity of the act does not in itself contradict the principle of effectiveness. Secondly, on the basis of the same principle, it is also precluded the application of national rules of evidence that are not sufficiently rigorous and, in fact, have the effect of shifting the burden of proof laid down in Article 16 EIR Recast—ECJ, *Nike*, para 29.

[65] ECJ, *Nike*, para 36.

reduces the scope for questioning the application of the *lex concursus* in certain situations—does not come as a surprise. It was expressly formulated in the *Virgos-Schmit* Report on the 1995 Insolvency Convention[66] or in various works of the legal scholars.[67] The equilibrium between *lex concursus* and *lex causae* is settled on a more accurate basis.

Generally, the *Nike* judgment confirms, if still necessary after *Lutz*, that in the operation of Article 16 EIR Recast the divergences between the Member States' legislations regarding the avoidance of fraudulent transactions may be used as a very effective, but sometimes unfair tool which limits the chances of success for the *actio pauliana* in cross-border insolvency proceedings.[68]

4.3.3 Vinyls Italy *Judgment*

The third judgment relevant for the interpretation of Article 16 EIR Recast dates from 8 June 2017[69] and it was a new opportunity for the Court of Justice to further clarify the requirements regarding its implementation.

4.3.3.1 The Procedural Regime of Article 16 EIR Recast

The first issue approached by the Court concerned the regime of the Article 16 EIR Recast—procedural exception subject to *lex fori* or particular exception subject to more liberal rules dictated by an autonomous interpretation of the Regulation. Considering that the rules on the form and time-limits for relying on Article 16 EIR Recast in the context of proceedings are similar in nature to those related to the

---

[66] See the *Virgos Schmit* Report, para 136, stating that '*By 'any means' it is understood that the act must not be capable of being challenged using either rules on insolvency or general rules of the national law applicable to the act*'.

[67] See for example Alexander 2009, pp. 16–17.

[68] Leandro 2017, p. 77; Keay 2017, p. 8; McCormack et al. 2016, p. 173.

[69] ECJ 8.6.2017—Case C-54/16 (*Vinyls Italy*). The case concerned two Italian companies that concluded a maritime charter contract for a vessel sailing under Italian flag; pursuant to the contract, Vinyls Italia has paid to Mediterranea approximately 450,000 Euros in a moment when its financial difficulties were notorious, even if formal insolvency proceedings were not yet initiated. After the opening of the insolvency proceedings, the insolvency practitioner brought an action for the payments' avoidance on the basis of the Italian law. Opposing to this action, Mediterranea requested application (on the basis of Article 13 EIR) of the provisions of English law, chosen by the parties to govern their contract and not allowing the challenge of the payments. In front of the national courts, particular discussions have arisen especially because the plaintiff claimed that Article 13 EIR (now Article 16 EIR Recast) must be understood as a procedural objection that should be invoked in the forms and within the time-limits laid down by the Italian law (*lex fori concursus*). Since this had not been the case in the dispute and the doubts on the correct interpretation of the provision still persisted, several questions were referred to the European Court of Justice for a preliminary ruling.

ways in which evidence is to be elicited or what evidence is to be admissible before the national court or to the probative value of the evidence, ECJ put forward the solution and the arguments from the *Nike* judgment on the articulation between the European and the national law of civil procedure. It considered that in the absence of a European harmonisation of the procedural rules related to the implementation of the text, the national legal order of the competent forum will be taken into account to that effect, in accordance with the principle of the procedural autonomy and in full compliance with the principles of equivalence and effectiveness.[70]

The consequence appears clearly: the form and time-limits for relying on Article 16 EIR Recast and the issue whether the court hearing the insolvency proceedings may apply that article of its own motion, come under the procedural law of the forum state.[71] Trying to explain also the irrelevance of the *lex causae* in the matter, the Court vaguely affirms that Article 16 '*do not aim to protect the litigant against the usual risk of having to defend himself in such proceedings, whether that be before the courts of the Member State on whose territory the person concerned resides or before the courts of another Member State, nor therefore, against the procedural law applied by the competent jurisdiction*'.[72] This answer is not an example of shining clarity in demonstration and do not succeed explaining properly, for example, why the *lex causae* can be applied for some procedural aspects (as in *Lutz* judgment), but not for others.[73] In its Opinion from 2 March 2017, Advocate general Szpunar seemed more persuasive on the delimitation of the scopes of application of the *lex fori processualis* and of the *lex causae*. Since the exception laid down in Article 16 EIR Recast concerns the judicial or procedural activity of the party which benefited from the detrimental act, its operation is closely connected with the way in which proceedings are conducted and cannot be detached from the entirety of the procedural rules in force in the forum State. For this reason, the way in which the corresponding procedural right is exercised and enforced must be subject to the law of the State whose courts have jurisdiction in the case,[74] while the *lex causae* should be consulted only as regards the provisions —including those having a procedural nature—that form part of the system for invalidating acts.[75] These precisions are well founded and could be followed as a possible point of reference in the future for the operation of Article 16.

---

[70] ECJ, *Vinyls*, para 26.

[71] ECJ, *Vinyls*, para 27.

[72] ECJ, *Vinyls*, para 31.

[73] It has nevertheless an undisputed effect: the *lex causae* will not be taken into account for any issue concerning the actions for the avoidance of fraudulent transactions.

[74] AG Opinion at paras 56, 57, 59.

[75] AG Opinion at para 60.

4.3.3.2   Application *in Concreto* of the *Lex Causae* and Burden of Proof

The Court also provided further guidance on the obligations of the defendant who
benefited from an act detrimental to all the creditors and on the application of the
lex causae provisions for upholding it, according to Article 16 EIR Recast.
Confirming and detailing its position in the *Nike* judgment, ECJ considered that this
provision would be deprived of its *effet utile* if the unchallengeable character of the
act on the basis of the *lex causae* should be taken into account only if that law
would not provide, in general or in the abstract, any means to challenge it.[76] On the
contrary, the requirement laid down in the Article 16 must be considered satisfied
when the detrimental act, although in principle capable of being challenged
according to *lex causae*, cannot effectively be invalidated in view of all the circumstances of the case. The solution rests on the objective pursued by the European
legislator in the field—the respect of the legitimate expectations of the parties—and
reflects *de novo* the particular equilibrium created between the *lex concursus* and *lex
causae* and between the different interests at stake. Confirming previous case law,
the burden of proofs is once more placed on the party relying on Article 16 EIR
Recast. The dismissal of the avoidance action will be possible only if the defendant
provides the proof that '*where the lex causae makes it possible to challenge an act
regarded as being detrimental, the conditions to be met in order for that challenge
to be upheld, which differ from those of the lex fori concursus, have not actually
been fulfilled*'.[77]

4.3.3.3   Large Place for the Party Autonomy

In the last part of the judgment, the Court of Justice approached a delicate issue: the
possibility of a deliberate use by the debtor (and its counterparty) of the flexible
rules of the Rome Convention[78] (now Rome I Regulation), and in particular of its
Article 3, which gives to the parties a large freedom to designate the law governing
the contract, on the one hand, and of the Article 16 EIR Recast, on the other hand,
in order to circumvent the mandatory rules of the *lex concursus* regarding the
avoidance of legal acts detrimental to all creditors.

The main concern of the Court was to ascertain the circumstances in which
Article 16 EIR Recast can be used. Based on textual and teleological arguments, the

---

[76] ECJ, *Vinyls*, para 38.

[77] ECJ, *Vinyls*, para 39.

[78] Since the referring court did not have jurisdiction to submit preliminary questions on the
interpretation of the Rome Convention, the ECJ was obliged to reformulate the preliminary
questions in order to assess its own jurisdiction (para 44). This technical issue put a mark on the
response provided. Although it excluded previously, from a temporal perspective, the application
of the Rome I Regulation in the dispute (para 42), the ECJ still referred expressly to it in its
judgment (paras 48, 49, 50). Also, through their generality, the Court's indications are undoubtfully effective also as regards the contracts entering into the scope of *Rome I* Regulation.

first part of its answer—accepting the applicability of this provision even when the parties, both established on the territory of a Member State, opted for the law of another Member State—come as no surprise. Trying to justify this position, the Court brought important details, that go beyond the question of the applicability of Article 16 EIR Recast and relates in fact to the determination of the *lex causae*. It stated that Article 3(3) of the Rome I Regulation has no role to play to this effect and even when all the other elements of a situation, apart from the choice by the parties of the applicable law, are located in a Member State other than the one whose law is chosen, the choice made by the parties must be the sole taken into account for the purposes of applying Article 16 EIR Recast.[79] The justification advanced for this relates to the mere absence, within the later text, of a derogation provision comparable to Article 3(3) of the Rome I Regulation.

4.3.3.4 Criticism

The appropriateness of this position may be doubted. To explain it more clearly, the Court accepts that if the issue in dispute would have been carried out in a purely contractual context (outside of insolvency), the application of the chosen law would have been possible only within the framework of Article 3(3) of the Rome I Regulation, a text which establishes important limits to the party autonomy with the aim of preventing them from circumventing the mandatory rules of a country, in wholly domestic situations, by the simple designation of a more liberal law.[80] However, due to the fact that the issue in dispute has arisen in an insolvency context, the law chosen by the parties to govern their contract may operate without other limitations and may be used to block an avoidance action admissible on the basis of *lex concursus*.

The solution is more than surprising. It endangers the coherent interpretation and functioning of the Rome I and EIR Recast, given the distinction established as regards the determination of the *lex causae* (*lex contractus*), depending on the context in which this law is designed to operate—outside or within insolvency proceedings. Moreover, its justifications are not very convincing. The Court referred to the wording of (now) Article 16 EIR Recast, which does not contain a derogating provision comparable to Article 3(3) of the Rome Convention or the Rome I Regulation, ignoring that such a provision was not in fact necessary. Article 16 EIR Recast makes an exception to the application of *lex concursus* in case of actions to set aside acts *'subject to the law of a Member State other than that of the State of the opening of proceedings'* and leaves to other instruments the task of determining the adequate provisions for determining the law governing those acts.[81]

---

[79] ECJ, *Vinyls*, paras 48–50.

[80] See Plender and Wilderspin 2009, paras 6.055–6.067, pp. 159–167; Mankowski in Magnus and Mankowski 2017, pp. 228 et seq, paras 374 et seq.

[81] See Leandro 2017, p. 80.

Under the pretext of the silence of the legislator, the Court established a new rule in the field, enhancing the role of the party autonomy. It allowed a free choice of the insolvency law applicable to avoidance transactions within the EU. Regrettably, except for the reference of the wording of Article 13 EIR, it did not explain why, as regards the relations between the parties, the *lex contractus* should be determined on the basis of all of the Rome I Regulation's provisions—Article 3(1), Article 3(3) or 3(4), Article 9—while in the context of insolvency proceedings, when the different interests at stake are much more compelling, only the chosen law[82] (Article 3 (1)) should be respected.

The consequences are important. The distinction established is likely to encourage the debtor to subtract assets from the insolvent estate or to aggravate its situation to the detriment of some of his creditors and go against the provisions of Recital 5 from the Preamble of EIR Recast. On the basis of the new jurisprudential rule, he will be permitted to conclude detrimental contracts for which he and his counterparties have elected foreign laws that do not allow or allow in restrictive conditions their avoidance in case of insolvency proceedings. The risk of utilisation of the provisions for fraudulent ends, already put forward by the doctrine,[83] becomes much more present.

4.3.3.5 Unsatisfactory Safeguard—The Prohibition of Fraudulent Practices

Certainly, preoccupied to limit the possible manipulations, the Court evoked the prohibition of the abuse of rights and of frauds (para 51) and tries to offer some guidance on the elements pertaining to their characterisation. Quite vague as regards the objective element of the abusive or fraudulent practices,[84] it insisted on the subjective, intentional element—the essential aim of the transactions concerned must be the obtention of an undue advantage which, in its turn, can be deduced from the purely artificial nature of the transactions concerned.[85] Further, discussing

---

[82] Actually, it is a matter of discussion whether for purely domestic contracts the parties are at liberty to choose the applicable law. Important authors consider that, when the parties adopt the law of a certain State for an internal contract, they only incorporate the content of the rules of the chosen law into their contract, that is otherwise governed by another law (objectively determined) —see Mankowski in Magnus and Mankowski 2017, p. 228, para 374 and p. 233, paras 392–393. The Court completely ignores such a debate and recognize a wide parties' autonomy as regards the contracts whose sort will be decided within insolvency proceedings.

[83] See the references cited *supra*, Sect. 4.2.3.2. More moderate on this risk, see Leandro 2017, p. 78.

[84] ECJ, *Vinyls*, para 52: '*First, with regard to the objective element, that finding requires that it must be apparent from a combination of objective circumstances that, despite formal observance of the conditions laid down by Community rules, the purpose of those rules has not been achieved*'; *actus reus* is far for being clearly defined.

[85] ECJ, *Vinyls*, paras 52–53.

in particular the application of Article 16 EIR Recast, it decided that this text could be disregarded only when there are no legitimate expectations to protect, because the parties artificially submitted the contract to the law of a specific Member State, with the primary aim to rely on that law just to circumvent the application of the *lex fori concursus* and not to solve their eventual contractual issues.[86]

This solution—imposing an appreciation *in concreto* of each situation—alleviates only partially the negative consequences described above. The Court ignored the fact that Article 3(3) of the *Rome I* Regulation or Rome Convention was precisely designed to prevent the parties from escaping the national (mandatory) law otherwise applicable to their contracts,[87] whether inspired or not by bad faith or fraudulent aims.[88] For the purely internal contracts, whatever the nature of the solution installed by Article 3(3)—proper choice of law rule or purely incorporation mechanism—the parties' freedom will always be restricted by the mandatory rules of the objectively applicable law. In *Vinyls*, the Court censored the 'automatic' operation of the Article 3(3) for purely domestic contracts analysed in the framework of an insolvency proceedings and imposed a verification *in concreto* of the existence of the fraud. The insolvency practitioner or the creditors interested in the success of the *actio pauliana* will be in a very delicate position. In order to avoid the application of a law that would not have been applicable outside insolvency proceedings (a law that the third party beneficiary of the act can invoke without any problems, following the *Vinyls* judgment), they will have to prove, in particular, the subjective element of the fraud—the fraudulent intent—a task very difficult if not impossible.[89] Because the standard of the fraud to prove becomes extremely high, the debtor will be once more encouraged to engage in possible manoeuvres of diminution of the estate, facilitated by the implementation of some strategies related to the law applicable to the acts concluded by him (*law shopping*), which increases the risk of dispute. Instead of trying to prevent the disputes through a restrictive interpretation of (now) Article 16 EIR Recast, with a proper consideration of the solutions found in the Rome I Regulation or the Rome Convention, dictated by coherence reasons, the Court reached an opposite result.

---

[86] ECJ, *Vinyls*, para 54.

[87] See Muir-Watt 2009, pp. 81–82; Bureau 1995, pp. 285 et seq; Plender and Wilderspin 2009, p. 160, para 6.057.

[88] Mankowski in Magnus and Mankowski 2017, p. 228, para 376.

[89] In general, the legal scholars consider that this subjective element could be deduced from the appreciation of the objective elements—see Audit 2006, p. 199, para 240. But in *Vinyls Italy* judgment, the Court clarified that the fraudulent intent cannot be presumed when the parties, having their head offices in a single Member State on whose territory all the other elements relevant to the situation in question are located, have designated the law of another Member State as the *lex contractus*—para 55.

4.4 Towards New Horizons?

4.4.1 Inconveniences of the Existing Rules

In spite of the indications given by the Court of Justice, the result of the implementation of the European rules concerning the actions to set aside detrimental acts is not necessarily a satisfactory one and it raises questions as to the opportunity of the decision of the European legislator to maintain unchanged in the EIR Recast the previous solutions. Assuming to have solved the jurisdictional problems, the insolvency practitioner will have to pay particular attention to the identification of the substantive governing law. If the *lex rei sitae, lex mercatus, lex laboris or lex registri* of a Member State are not applicable (according to Articles 11, 12, 13 or 14 EIR Recast), he will certainly have to comply with the avoidance provisions of the *lex concursus*. Subsequently and complementarily, for every transaction he intends to set aside (avoidable according to the *lex concursus*), he will have to determine also the law governing that transaction (a law sometimes strategically chosen) and those of its provisions which could impair the success of the *actio pauliana*. This entrains important inconveniences in terms of costs, delays and uncertainties and has a potential discouraging effect as regards the challenge of the transactions.

Although the cumulative application of two laws for each detrimental transaction is not what was originally intended by the European legislator, the result of the case law of the European Court of Justice is very close to this. In fact, in order to obtain the avoidance, the practitioner will have to comply with the requirements of the most severe of the two laws (*lex concursus* and *lex causae*), both as regards the merits and (some of) the procedural aspects. These doubled standards seriously affect the efficacy of States' laws regarding the avoidance of detrimental acts and undermine, in the benefit of the party autonomy, the political goals which inspire these laws—mainly, the equity and the respect of the priority rules in the distributions. This situation is not necessarily consistent with the European objectives in this field—maximisation of chances of recovery for the debtor, enhanced promotion of the coherence, of the efficiency and effectiveness in the insolvency proceedings.

It is clear, the solutions found in the Regulation superposed on the differences existing between the Member States' legislations in the field of insolvency, are a great source of complexity and uncertainty as regards the results of the avoidance actions in cases with foreign elements.[90] For an improvement, a legislative modification was and is necessary.

---

[90] Leandro 2017, p. 81.

4.4.2 Reforms of the Conflicts of Law Rules

Despite this need, in the recast process, the European legislator decided not to intervene. The reasons for the inaction can be related to the fact that some of the inconveniences of the existing rules were not really perceived until recently, with the multiplication of the relevant ECJ's case law on the matter. More importantly, they might be also found in the limits of a reform at a conflict of laws level. The European legislator could have envisaged a reform of the existing texts, the range of alternatives available being quite broad. A possible rule could have allowed the application of (solely) the *lex concursus* or of the (solely) *lex causae*. Also, it could have allowed the application of the law chosen by the insolvency practitioner or the application of the law with which the situation is most closely connected.

Each of these options implies however serious drawbacks.[91] The doctrine already suggested the application of the sole *lex concursus* (and the suppression of the Article 13 EIR) in the discussions concerning the recent reform.[92] This solution is likely to simplify the mission of the insolvency practitioner (and probably also of the competent judge) and brings more certainty in the field, while reinforcing the principle of the universality of the proceedings. Regrettably, it also appears as unfair to the third-party beneficiary of the challenged act, who will not be able to rely on the law governing it, and this is the reason why, following the recommendation from the Hess Report,[93] the EIR Recast kept the provision unchanged. The application of the sole *lex causae* is not fully satisfactory either. Such a solution may correspond to the concerns and expectations of the third parties, but presents important inconveniences in terms of costs, delays and complexity generated by the insolvency practitioner's obligation to comply with each of the laws governing the various acts that he wants to set aside. Finally, given the unpredictability and the uncertainties generated, the other two alternatives advanced are neither more adequate from the perspective of the different interests at stake.[94] Once again, in the light of this, the solution in the EIR Recast is a reflection of a compromise designed to equilibrate the different interests at stake in the light of the widely differing substantive laws on the matter.

4.4.3 Harmonisation of the Substantive Avoidance Laws

In these conditions, the action at another level—that of the substantive law—might be envisaged in the future as a viable alternative[95] or at least as a prerequisite for the

---

[91] Keay 2017, pp. 10–11.

[92] See for example Kolmann 2011, p. 9; Carballo Piñeiro 2014, p. 212.

[93] Pfeiffer 2013, pp. 313–314.

[94] See Keay 2017, p. 10.

[95] See Vallens 2015, p. 761; Keay 2017, p. 12; McCormack et al. 2016, pp. 177 et seq. In general, on the inconveniences raised by the divergences existing between the Member States' legislations

reforms in the conflict of laws field. In fact, the harmonisation of the substantive law has been widely followed until now by the European legislator in matters related to commercial law, with successful outcomes.[96] Even if the insolvency law is highly influenced by particular choices of national politics, which renders improbable at this moment a full harmonisation of this area of law in the European Union, specific interventions on the aspects having (the most) perturbing effects are worthwhile and also perfectly feasible.[97] Since the differences between the substantive legislations of the Member States are important and a common (European) position is not yet crystalized on the aims and objectives of the future uniform norms, the technical difficulties will not be missing.[98]

However, they are not insurmountable[99] and the efforts made to overcome them would be greatly rewarded. At least as regards the issue of the avoidance of transactions detrimental to the creditors in insolvency proceedings, a set of harmonised rules at the European Union level would bring more efficiency, fairness and coherence in the proceedings. The costs related to the identification and application of different avoidance laws (some of them foreign) will diminish and the avoidance actions will be dealt in a timelier manner; the disputes regarding precisely the law governing the avoidance actions will rarely arise. The consecration of a set of harmonized avoidance rules would ensure a more egalitarian and fair treatment for those interested, regardless of the place where the proceedings were initiated or of the law governing the transactions subject to the avoidance action. The risks of *forum shopping* and *law shopping*—the incentives for the debtor to

---

in the field of insolvency (restrictions on the free movement, unfair competitive advantages and/or disadvantages, difficulties of the companies in carrying out cross-border activities), see the study of INSOL Europe 2010, pp. 7–26.

[96] For an overview of the European regulations and directives adopted in the field of corporate law, see Engammare and Mustaki 2009.

[97] INSOL Europe has already provided a comprehensive list of problems which might occur in the absence of harmonized rules on insolvency. It also identified some specific areas where harmonisation of insolvency law at EU level is worthwhile and achievable; the provisions regarding the avoidance actions are among them—INSOL Europe 2010, pp. 26–29, specially at p. 27.

[98] For a detailed presentation of the technical difficulties that may be generated by the harmonisation process in the field of the insolvency law, see Keay 2017, pp. 19–20.

[99] See de Weijs 2011, formulating a detailed proposal for a European rule on transaction avoidance in insolvencies. The proposal distinguishes between three categories of detrimental acts (legal acts compromising the integrity of the estate, preferences and shareholder loans and guarantees), each of them subdivided into two subcategories, and favours mainly objective criteria for avoidance actions. See INSOL Europe with the following suggestions: '*(1) the abolition of any reference to the law of the contract with respect to the avoidance actions under Article 13 of the EC Regulation No 1346/2000; (2) a distinction must be made where a transaction is with a connected party; (3) the provision of a minimum period of, for example, 90 days for detrimental acts with unconnected parties and one year for connected parties; (4) a minimum list of actions which are subject to possible annulment of the transactions involved; (5) bad faith requirements with respect to the insolvent debtor and/or the other party; (6) the burden of proof with respect to detriment and bad faith and (7) the fact of such actions may only be brought by the office holder on behalf of the estate*' (p. 20).

move its COMI or for the parties to designate a particular law to govern their legal relationship, in order to benefit from a more favourable avoidance law—will also decrease. Finally, a harmonised set of avoidance provisions at the European Union level would correct the existing drawbacks of the European regulations on the issue and would better respond to the legitimate expectations of the interested parties in terms of predictability, stability, accessibility of law and legal certainty. So maybe is time for the European legislator to prepare to act again.

References

Alexander J (2009) Avoid the choice or choose to avoid? The European Framework for Choice of Avoidance Law and the Quest to Make it Sensible. https://ssrn.com/abstract=1410157. Accessed 28 January 2019

Audit B (2006) Droit international privé. Economica, Paris

Bork R (2017) Clash of Principles: Equal Treatment of Creditors vs. Protection of Trust in European Transactions Avoidance Laws (CERIL Report on Transactions Avoidance Laws 2017/1). http://www.ceril.eu/uploads/files/20170926-ceril-report-2017-1-final.pdf. Accessed 28 January 2019

Bureau D (1995) L'influence de la volonté individuelle sur les conflits de lois. In: Mélanges en hommage à F. Terré. Dalloz, Paris, pp 285–306

Bureau D (2002) La fin d'un îlot de résistance - le règlement du Conseil relatif aux procédures d'insolvabilité. Rev.Crit. DIP (3):613–679

Carballo Pinero L (2010) Vis Attractiva Concursus in the European Union: Its Development by the European Court of Justice. InDret (3):1–29. https://ssrn.com/abstract=2482030. Accessed 28 January 2019

Carballo Piñeiro L (2014) Towards the Reform of the European Insolvency Regulation: Codification Rather than Modification. Nederlands Internationaal Privaatrecht (NIPR) 32(2):207–215

Dammann R, Bleicher V (2014) Interrogations sur les effets extraterritoriaux du règlement d'insolvabilité no 1346/2000/CE. Recueil Dalloz, Paris, pp 1708–1714

Dammann R, Pigot M (2016) L'application de l'Article 13 du règlement EC 1346/2000 aux actions en nullité de la période suspecte. Recueil Dalloz, Paris, pp 525–532

De Weijs R (2011) Towards an Objective European Rule on Transaction Avoidance in Insolvencies. Amsterdam Law School Legal Studies Research Paper No. 2011-03. https://papers.ssrn.com/sol3/papers.cfm?abstract_id=1817663. Accessed 28 January 2019

Eidenmuller H (2009) Abuse of law in the context of European insolvency law. ECFR (1): 1–28. https://epub.ub.uni-muenchen.de/25813/1/oa_25813.pdf. Accessed 28 January 2019

Engammare V, Mustaki G (2009) Droit européen des sociétés. Helbing & Lichtenhahn, Basel

Fritz D (2011) Harmonisation of Insolvency Law at EU Level: Avoidance Actions and Rules on Contracts. Briefing note requested by the European Parliament's Committee on Legal Affairs. http://www.europarl.europa.eu/RegData/etudes/note/join/2011/432767/IPOL-JURI_NT(2011)432767_EN.pdf. Accessed 28 January 2019

Gurrea-Martínez A (2018) The Avoidance of Pre-Bankruptcy Transactions: An Economic and Comparative Approach. Chicago-Kent Law Review, 93(3):711–750. https://ssrn.com/abstract=2845101. Accessed 28 January 2019

INSOL Europe (2010) Harmonisation of Insolvency law at EU Level. Document requested by the European Parliament's Committee on Legal Affairs. http://www.eesc.europa.eu/resources/docs/ipol-juri_nt2010419633_en.pdf. Accessed 28 January 2019

Jault Seseke F, Robine D (2014) L'application du règlement insolvabilité dans les relations avec un Etat tiers. Recueil Dalloz, Paris, pp 915–918

Keay A (2017) The harmonisation of the avoidance rules in the European Union Insolvencies. ICLQ 66(1):79–105. https://doi.org/10.1017/s0020589316000518. http://eprints.whiterose.ac.uk/103627/. Accessed 29 January 2019

Kolmann S (2011) Thoughts on the governing insolvency law. http://www.eir-reform.eu/uploads/PDF/AMMEND_Kolmann.pdf. Accessed January 2015 (link no longer active)

Leandro A (2017) Harmonisation and Avoidance Disputes against the Background of the European Insolvency Regulation. In: Gant J (ed) Harmonisation of European Insolvency Law. INSOL-Europe, Nottingham, pp 71–81

Linna T (2014) Actio Pauliana – Actio europensis? Some Cross-Border Insolvency Issues. J. of PIL 10:69–87. https://doi.org/10.5235/17441048.10.1.69

Linna T (2015) Actio pauliana and res judicata in EU insolvency proceedings. J. of PIL 11:568–584. https://doi.org/10.1080/17441048.2015.1102472

Magnus U, Mankowski P (2017) Rome I Regulation. Otto Schmidt, Cologne

McCormack G (2009) Jurisdictional Competition and Forum Shopping in Insolvency Proceedings. Cambridge Law Journal, 68(1): 169–197. https://doi.org/10.1017/s0008197309000075

McCormack G, Keay A, Brown S, Dahlgreen J (2016) Study on a new approach to business failure and insolvency. Comparative legal analysis of the Member States' relevant provisions and practices. Study commissioned by the European Commission, DG Justice and Consumers. https://publications.europa.eu/en/publication-detail/-/publication/3eb2f832-47f3-11e6-9c64-01aa75ed71a1/language-en. Accessed 28 January 2019

Menjucq M (2005) L'apport du droit communautaire au règlement des faillites internationales. In: Travaux du Comité français de droit international privé 2002–2004. Pedone, Paris, pp 35–63

Moss G, Fletcher IF, Isaacs I (2009) The EC Regulation on insolvency proceedings. A commentary and Annotated Guide. OUP, Oxford

Muir-Watt H (2009) Le principe d'autonomie entre libéralisme et néo-libéralisme. In: Fallon M et al (eds) La matière civile et commerciale, socle d'un code européen de droit international privé. Dalloz, Paris, pp 77–92

Pfeiffer P (2013) Article 13 EIR: Avoidance, Avoidability and Voidness. In: Hess B et al (eds) External Evaluations of Regulation No 1346/2000/EC on Insolvency Proceedings, JUST/2011/JVC/PR/0049/A4.   https://www.mpi.lu/uploads/media/evaluation_insolvency_en.pdf Accessed 29 January 2019

Plender R, Wilderspin M (2009) The European Private International Law of Obligations. Sweet and Maxwell, London

Pretelli I (2011) Cross-Border Credit Protection Against Fraudulent Transfers of Assets: Actio Pauliana in the Conflict of Laws. Yearbook of PIL 13:589–640. https://papers.ssrn.com/sol3/papers.cfm?abstract_id=2148307. Accessed 28 January 2019

UNCITRAL (2004) Legislative Guide on Insolvency Law. https://www.uncitral.org/pdf/english/texts/insolven/05-80722_Ebook.pdf. Accessed 28 January 2019

Vallens JL (2015) Actions en nullité et procédures transfrontalières. RTD Com (3):755–759

Veder M (2011) Applicable law, in particular security rights. In: The future of the European Insolvency   Regulation.   http://www.eir-reform.eu/uploads/papers/PAPER%204-3.pdf. Accessed January 2015 (link no longer active)

Virgos M, Schmit E (1995) Report on the Convention on Insolvency Proceedings from 23 November 1995, Council Doc. No 6500/1/96 REV 1 DRS CFC

Chapter 5
Cooperation and Communication Between Parties in the Management of Cross-Border Parallel Proceedings Under the European Insolvency Regulation Recast

Ilaria Queirolo and Stefano Dominelli

Contents

Ilaria Queirolo (Sects. 5.1, 5.2, 5.4, 5.5), Full Professor of International Law, University of Genoa; Stefano Dominelli (Sects. 5.3, 5.6), Researcher in International Law, University of Genoa.

I. Queirolo (✉) · S. Dominelli (✉)
International Law, University of Genoa, Piazzale E. Brignole 3a, Genoa 16125, Italy
e-mail: Ilaria.Queirolo@unige.it

S. Dominelli
e-mail: stefano.dominelli@edu.unige.it

© T.M.C. ASSER PRESS and the authors 2020
V. Lazić and S. Stuij (eds.), *Recasting the Insolvency Regulation*, Short Studies in Private International Law,
https://doi.org/10.1007/978-94-6265-363-4_5

Abstract Regulation (EU) 2015/848 of the European Parliament and of the Council of 20 May 2015 on insolvency proceedings implements and introduces new substantive obligations for insolvency practitioners as regards cooperation and communication. Whereas such duties between liquidators under the previous legal framework already existed, new ones are added, and new actors are bound by them. The present work wishes to explore some of the main theoretical and practical shortcomings in the application of those rules.

Keywords Cross-Border Insolvency · European Insolvency Regulation · European Judicial Space · Cooperation · Parallel Proceedings · Best Practices

5.1 The Necessity for Coordination of Insolvency Proceedings with Cross-Border Elements Within the European Judicial Space

The construction and development of the internal market has been the driving force of European integration ever since the creation of the first European Communities. Not only rules on freedom of establishment and rules on providing services are necessary to attain such a goal. The protection of the European market also requires specific rules to tackle the pathologic moment of economic activities, i.e. insolvency.[1] Where harmonisation in substantive insolvency law has proven to be more difficult for the Member States of the European Union,[2] judicial cooperation under current Article 81 TFEU has proven to be more acceptable as regards allocation of jurisdiction, applicable law and recognition and enforcement of decisions. Harmonised solutions at the private international law level are necessary for a better management of cross-border insolvency proceedings.

Historically, EU private international law rules *lato sensu* on the subject matter compose the 'universality' and the 'territoriality' models to allocate international jurisdiction.[3] This leads to the consequence that multiple proceedings against the

---

[1] Cf. Villata 2018, p. 89.

[2] In 2011 the European Parliament requested the European Commission to submit proposals for the development of a European Union corporate insolvency (European Parliament resolution of 15 November 2011, Insolvency proceedings in the context of EU company law with recommendations to the Commission on insolvency proceedings in the context of EU company law, in OJ C 153E, 31.5.2013, p. 1). More recently, a piece of legislation is discussed to adopt harmonized rules (Proposal for a Directive of the European Parliament and of the Council on preventive restructuring frameworks, second chance and measures to increase the efficiency of restructuring, insolvency and discharge procedures and amending Directive 2012/30/EU, COM 2016(0723) final).

[3] In addition to the chapters of this *Volume*, see Enriques 1934, p. 145 ff; Lupone 1995, p. 56; Daniele 1987, p. 4; Fumagalli 2018, p. 182; Queirolo 2007, p. 13; Kindler 2018, p. 1934; Paulus 2017, p. 92; Mäsch 2015a (Einleitung), p. 1072.

same debtor can be opened in different Member States. It was apparent that coordination between the several proceedings was a necessity to avoid a disaggregated management of assets to the detriment of both the debtor and creditors.[4] To that end, the first European Insolvency Regulation[5] provided rules for communication and cooperation between insolvency office holders,[6] and rules for unilateral coordination of the main insolvency practitioner.[7] Nonetheless, the legal framework was criticised for its narrow personal scope of application,[8] as only professionals and not courts were subject to the provision, and for the general structure of the regulation itself—as the main proceedings could have had the aim to rescue the company, whilst secondary proceedings were only winding-up in nature.[9] To better ensure proper coordinated management of cross-border insolvency proceedings the regulation has been recast[10] and cooperation duties have been extended. However, the success of the reform will prove only in time given that—as shall be addressed—the current legal framework raises a number of theoretical and applicative questions.[11]

5.2 Setting Coordination Following Imposition and Following Cooperation Apart

If cooperation between parallel insolvency proceedings opened against the same debtor is a necessity to ensure an overall proper management of insolvency assets, 'coordination' in a wider sense does not necessarily recognise the same prerogatives to all actors and subjects of proceedings.

---

[4] Leandro 2017, p. 939; Virgós and Garcimartín 2004, p. 225; Mankowski 2016a (Article 41), para 1; Arnold 2015, p. 96; Bork 2017, p. 44. On the contrary, some might argue differently from the perspective of one State only, since often insolvency laws were considered as the expression of domestic rules for the protection of public interests (Carbone 2004, p. 93). As noted by Farley 2009, p. 76, '[i]t is only relatively recently that the insolvency profession and the courts have been able to work toward a system that pays more attention to interests of the stakeholders than to issues of the national sovereignty of the jurisdictions involved'. Cf. Schmüser 2009, p. 46.

[5] Council regulation (EC) No. 1346/2000 of 29 May 2000 on insolvency proceedings, in OJ L 160, 30.6.2000, p. 1 (European Insolvency Regulation).

[6] European Insolvency Regulation, Article 31.

[7] See, for example, European Insolvency Regulation, Articles 33, and 34.

[8] See in particular Moss and Smith 2016, p. 486, and Pannen and Riedermann 2007 (Article 31), p. 463. However, in the case law, OLG Wien (AT) 09.11.2004—28 R 225/04w, in *Neue Zeitschrift für Insolvenz-und Sanierungsrecht*, 2005, p. 56 ff excluded the possibility to extend the cooperation duty also to the level of court-to-court cooperation.

[9] Crawford and Carruthers 2015, p. 662.

[10] Regulation (EU) 2015/848 of the European Parliament and of the Council of 20 May 2015 on insolvency proceedings, in OJ L 141, 5.6.2015, p. 19 (EIR Recast).

[11] Cfr. Oberhammer et al. 2016, p. 119; Bewick 2015, p. 188; Van Calster 2016, p. 749; Thole and Dueñas 2016, p. 218; McCormack 2015, p. 143, and Fazzini 2015, p. 907.

The European Insolvency Regulation Recast (EIR Recast) grants the sole administrator of the main insolvency proceedings, whose appointment has effects in all Member States without any particular procedure,[12] the possibility to influence secondary proceedings. In the first place, only the principal administrator has the right to give an undertaking in order to avoid opening of secondary proceedings.[13] The main insolvency practitioner is immediately informed of requests for opening secondary proceedings,[14] which he can eventually challenge should their opening not comply with the regulation.[15]

In the second place, once secondary proceedings have been opened, the main insolvency practitioner may require a (renewable) three months stay of the process of realisation of assets in those secondary proceedings—with the peculiar feature that if the main insolvency practitioner takes measures to ensure protection of local creditors requested by the local court, the stay must be granted, as the sole criterion to reject the requested stay is the *manifest* absence of interest to the creditors in the main proceedings.[16]

Additionally, only the main insolvency practitioner may propose restructuring plans in secondary proceedings, to the extent the local law permits closure of proceedings in such a way.[17] No similar power is granted to secondary insolvency practitioners, should more secondary proceedings be opened—nor to the secondary insolvency practitioner to be exercised in the context of the main one.

Lastly, remaining assets of secondary proceedings are to be transferred to the main insolvency practitioner.[18] Nonetheless, this should be of reduced practical importance, as the opening of an insolvency or pre-insolvency procedures postulates the impossibility for the debtor to pay all his debts.

5.2.1   Preliminary Considerations: The Prevalence of the Main Insolvency Proceedings in Matters of 'Coordination' Latu Sensu

The possibility for the main insolvency practitioner to 'obtain' coordination where a number of conditions are met, is grounded upon the idea that the main proceedings —being the one opened in the Member State of the centre of main interests of the debtor, and being the one that absent secondary proceedings would have had

---

[12] EIR Recast, Article 21.
[13] *Ibidem*, Article 36.
[14] *Ibidem*, Article 38.
[15] *Ibidem*, Article 39.
[16] *Ibidem*, Article 46.
[17] *Ibidem*, Article 47.
[18] *Ibidem*, Article 49.

universal effects within the European judicial space—should not be prejudiced by the opening of local procedures.

The idea of a predominance of the main proceedings[19] in matters of coordination does not find a clear transposition in the terminology used by the regulation in matters of 'collaborative coordination'. This circumstance, taken alone should however not be sufficient to disregard what appears to be the general object of the instrument—i.e. coordination of local proceedings with the universal proceedings.

5.2.2 The Prevalence of the Main Insolvency Proceedings in Matters of 'Coordination' Latu Sensu: A Critique

The predominance of the main proceedings over secondary ones, granting a privileged position of the main insolvency practitioner, rests upon the idea that the universal proceedings opened at the centre of main interest of the debtor should be the gravity of actions in the European judicial space as most probably the most significant assets are located in that Member State. There are, however, scenarios where this might not necessarily be true.

In the first place, even if the assets of the main insolvency proceedings might be more relevant in comparison to those of a secondary proceedings, should multiple secondary proceedings be opened, the total value of such assets might outweigh those of the main.[20]

In the second place, problematic scenarios, where the facts depart from the general principle, are connected with the localization of the COMI, thus the opening of the main insolvency proceedings. Courts of the main insolvency proceedings could localise the COMI in a State that is not the real State of the COMI, or in a State other than the one where significant investments are made. Such an opening judgment would have immediate effects in all other Member States,[21] whose courts would be left with the possibility either to open only a secondary proceedings or to make recourse to the public policy exception to avoid recognition and enforcement.[22]

Such a last scenario can be detected in the case law of some Member States, in particular where group of companies are subject to insolvency proceedings. For example, French courts have localised the COMI of a company of a group in France, i.e. where the mother company had its COMI. Nonetheless, the controlled

---

[19] EIR Recast, recital 48. Cf. Starace 2002, p. 302; Virgós and Garcimartín 2004, p. 225; Wessels 2016a (Article 41), p. 462; Hess 2010, p. 524; Pannen and Riedermann 2007 (Article 31), p. 459; Laukemann 2016, p. 380; Leandro 2014, p. 319; Israël 2005, p. 304; Bork and Mangano 2016, p. 206; Leandro 2017, p. 944; Leandro 2018, p. 119; Queirolo and Dominelli 2017a (Cooperation), p. 139. In the case law, CJEU 22 November 2012, *Bank Handlowy w Warszawie SA and PPHU «ADAX»/Ryszard Adamiak v Christianapol sp. z o.o.*, Case C-116/11.

[20] Mankowski 2016a (Article 41), para 47.

[21] EIR Recast, Article 19.

[22] *Ibidem*, Article 21.

business only had activities and assets in Italy, where courts opened a secondary proceedings. This led to the consequence that all assets where managed only by the insolvency practitioner in the secondary proceedings. Of course, co-existence of a main insolvency practitioner and a secondary insolvency practitioner still required application of cooperation duties.[23]

5.3 Cooperation Between Parties in Insolvency Proceedings

As opposed to other fields, not only is communication a necessity in insolvency law, but *quick* communication is fundamental as '*Insolvency proceedings generally involve dealing with matters subject to the immediacy of real time litigation as opposed to autopsy litigation which can be more leisurely pursued*'.[24] Article 41 EIR Recast confirms the pre-existing obligation upon practitioners to '*cooperate and communicate*'. Similar obligations are set upon courts for their relationships (Article 42), and between practitioners and courts (Article 43). Moreover, similar duties are imposed upon main practitioners appointed in insolvency proceedings opened against different debtors that are part of a group of companies (Article 56). Additionally, a new 'officer' is established, that of the '*coordinator*', whose task is to seek coordination between practitioners in the context of autonomous proceedings opened against different debtors of group (Article 61).

In this sense, the current legal framework has an extended scope of application in comparison to the former.[25]

5.3.1 The Obligation to Cooperate and Communicate in the EIR Recast

The first issue practitioners might encounter in the application of the regulation lies in the circumstance that duties are vaguely defined.[26] No clear definition of

---

[23] Cass. 29 ottobre 2015, n. 22093, Soc. Illochroma Italia c. S., in *Fallimento*, 2016, p. 829, on which see Queirolo and Dominelli 2017b (Italian Report), p. 350.

[24] Farley 1997, p. 237.

[25] Bork and Mangano 2016, p. 204; Santen 2015, p. 232 ff; and Wessels 2016a (Article 41), p. 458. Additionally, it must necessarily be pointed out that some Member States, following the first insolvency regulation, adopted domestic laws to clearly regulate the duty of cooperation between insolvency office holders. In this sense, for example, see Artículo 227. Obligaciones de cooperación, Ley 22/2003, «BOE» núm. 164, de 10/07/2003, and §357 InsO.

[26] Cf already Report from the Commission to the European Parliament, the Council and the European Economic and Social Committee on the application of Council Regulation (EC) No. 1346/2000 of 29 May 2000 on insolvency proceedings (COM(2012) 743 final), p. 14.

'cooperation' and 'communication' is given, and simple indications are only given by way of a non-exhaustive list of examples.

The necessity for a clear determination of the content of the obligations to communicate, coordinate, and cooperate, defined as the *'three C-s concept'*[27] has led part of legal scholars[28] to propose a substantive definition of the terms which seems clear enough to appreciate the differences, and the obligations that follow from such a classification. Where European rules refers to 'communication', the lowest threshold of collaboration should be intended, which is limited to exchange of (relevant) information. Where European rules refer to 'coordination', a mid-threshold of collaboration is intended, since here the parties involved in the management of cross-border insolvency proceedings are to work together for the realisation of shared and specific purposes.[29] On the contrary, 'cooperation' should refer to the highest threshold of collaboration between the interested parties, since these should cooperate together towards then same end.[30]

5.3.2 The Obligation to Cooperate and Communicate: From Theory to Practice

A duty to cooperate is imposed,[31] but practical results will highly depend on the will and skills of practitioners.

The first obligation is to exchange information.[32] No particular formality is imposed, the only limit being the protection of confidential data.[33] Current practice is not conclusive in the identification of information to be protected, whilst being undisputed that information already disseminated in the public must be surrendered.[34] Confidential and commercially relevant information could be kept as being

---

[27] Santen 2015, p. 230, and Pannen and Riedermann 2007 (Article 31), p. 460.

[28] Santen 2015, p. 230.

[29] *Ibidem*, p. 231.

[30] *Ibidem*.

[31] Cf. Leandro 2014, p. 318; Crawford and Carruthers 2015, p. 659, fn 197, and CJEU 22 November 2012, *Bank Handlowy w Warszawie SA and PPHU «ADAX»/Ryszard Adamiak* v *Christianapol sp. z o.o.*, Case C-116/11.

[32] EIR Recast, Article 41, and Article 56 for cooperation between practitioners in case of parallel proceedings opened against different debtors of a group of companies.

[33] Mankowski 2016a (Article 41), para 22 ff, and para 40, in similar terms, as to the modalities of cooperation.

[34] This has, for example, been clearly written in the Cross-Border Insolvency Protocol for the Lehman Brothers Group of Companies (available online), where, at Article 4.3. on Communication and Access to Data and Information Among Official Representatives, it can be read that '[t]*o facilitate access to inform action, Official Representatives should make available to each other, upon request, any information that is publicly available in their respective Fora; and may, where permitted under applicable laws, share non-public information with other Official Representatives, subject to appropriate confidentiality arrangements and all privileges under the*

sensible.[35] However, a list of cases in which a piece of information is not to be considered as 'confidential', is missing. Assuming that smooth exchange of relevant information is the rule, the question arises what the parties can share with each other. Article 41(2)(a) EIR Recast, and contrary to Article 56(2)(1),[36] offers an open[37] list, pointing to '*any progress made in lodging and verifying claims and all measures aimed at rescuing or restructuring the debtor, or at terminating the proceedings*'.[38] Practices have led to agreements clearly providing for reasonable request all books, records, reports and opinions of experts other than those of legal counsel.[39] Quick and cost-effective informal exchange of information is crucial, if informality is sufficient for the purposes of the single case.[40] Both provisions mention that exchange of information should take place 'as soon as possible' (thus without specifying 'when'[41]): no formalities, to be added to possible necessary informal translations, should be imposed to the detriment of a speedy exchange. However, should the information be used in court, documents should be sent so as to respect rules of evidence in the court where they are to be exhibited.

Under Article 42 EIR Recast, courts also have a duty to exchange information between themselves. Here, the principle of direct communication leads to reject the use of international rogatory commissions for courts to communicate.[42] The regulation states that courts shall ensure '*communication of information by any means considered*' appropriate. The TRI Leiden EU Cross-Border Insolvency

---

applicable rules of evidence'. Similarly, Queen's Bench of Alberta, Calpine Canada Energy Ltd, et al., Act No. 0501-17864, Section 17.

[35] Wessels and Virgós 2007, guideline 7.5.

[36] This provision in fact, being more general in nature, only provides that practitioners shall '*communicate to each other any information which may be relevant to the other proceedings*'.

[37] Whose non-exhaustive nature is confirmed by the use of the term 'in particular'.

[38] On practical examples of information to be exchanged, ranging from an overview of the assets to the docket number of the procedure, see Mäsch 2015b (Article 31), p. 1211; Virgós and Garcimartín 2004, p. 233; Wessels 2016a (Article 41), p. 465.

[39] Commodore Electronics Limited, and Commodore International Electric (available on the International Insolvency Institute website).

[40] Also suggesting the use of IT in communication to ensure prompt exchange of information, see Adriaanse et al. 2014, Principle 5.

[41] What is not directly addressed is 'when' liquidators should exchange relevant information. Reference to highest professional standards, against the background of the circumstances and difficulties of the case, such as translation issues, should be made (on this point, see Wessels 2016a (Article 41), p. 489, and Pannen and Riedermann 2007 (Article 31), p. 464). Some have also suggested that liquidators must inform all known parties about their own appointment within four days from the appointment itself (Adriaanse et al. 2014, Principle 5). See also Mankowski 2016a (Article 41), para 25.

[42] Schmidt 2016a (Article 57), p. 601. Cfr. also Superior Court of Canada, Province of Quebec, District of Montreal, Case 500-11-036133-094, July 28, 2009, Order Approving a Cross-Border Court to Court Protocol, in Abitibobowater Inc., Section 11. However, as argued by Moss and Smith 2016, p. 484, whereas the regulation wishes to avoid international rogatory, courts can freely decide whether they should communicate directly, or through legal counsels or autonomous bodies.

Court-to-Court Cooperation Guidelines highlight in particular that communication should ensure respect of procedures applicable in each interested State,[43] and it may take place by sending or transmitting (directly or through legal counsel) copies of formal orders, judgments, opinions, etc., or by way of e-links[44] (even though these last appear to be more suited to those cases that do not present particular complexities[45]). Not only should exchange of information cover relevant facts, substantive (in particular where one court is called to apply the foreign law) and procedural laws, but any information related to any pleading filed with one court, as well as schedules of hearings, should be communicated.[46]

The second obligation is for cooperation and coordination—between insolvency practitioners under Article 41 EIR Recast, between courts (Article 42), and between practitioners and courts (Article 43), with similar prescriptions for cases of multiple proceedings opened against different debtors of a group of companies (Article 56). Under the notion of 'coordination', practitioners shall '*explore the possibility of restructuring the debtor and, where such a possibility exists, coordinate the elaboration and implementation of a restructuring plan*'.[47] Additionally, practitioners shall '*coordinate the administration of the realization or use of the debtor's assets and affairs*'.[48]

For court to court cooperation and coordination the regulation provides an open[49] list as well. Courts can coordinate (i) the appointment of insolvency practitioners (even appoint the same person as insolvency practitioner in different proceedings,[50] should this be feasible[51]); (ii) coordinate the administration and

---

[43] TRI Leiden EU Cross-Border Insolvency Court-to-Court Cooperation Guidelines, Guideline 2.1, on which see Santen 2015, p. 238.

[44] TRI Leiden EU Cross-Border Insolvency Court-to-Court Cooperation Guidelines, Guideline 7.

[45] Farley 2009, p. 81. Specifically on e-links, see also TRI Leiden EU Cross-Border Insolvency Court-to-Court Cooperation Guidelines, Guideline 8.

[46] Superior Court of Canada, Province of Quebec, District of Montreal, Case 500-11-036133-094, July 28, 2009, Order Approving a Cross-Border Court to Court Protocol, in Abitibobowater Inc., Section 23.

[47] EIR Recast, Article 41, and Article 56. There have also been cases in Europe of agreements between liquidators who have sought cooperation for the sales of the debtor's assets. For a study on the practice in the BCCI Group, see Shandro 1998, p. 64.

[48] Similarly, see EIR Recast, Article 56(2)(b).

[49] 2006 UNCITRAL Practice Guide on Cross-Border Insolvency Cooperation, p. 23; Superior Court of Canada, Province of Quebec, District of Montreal, Case 500-11-036133-094, July 28, 2009, Order Approving a Cross-Border Court to Court Protocol, in Abitibobowater Inc., Section 11; In Re Barzel Industries et al., US Bankruptcy Court for the District of Delaware, Case No. 09-13204, Section 15.

[50] Mankowski 2016b (Article 42), para 19. Nonetheless, it must necessarily be outlined that such a possibility is not directly envisaged in the text of the articles of the regulation, but is rather contained as explanation in recital 50.

[51] Such a single person would need to have qualifications in all the interested jurisdictions. Additionally, as noted by Bewick 2015, p. 184, practical issues are likely to emerge in such a scenario, as insolvency law is strictly interconnected with a number of areas of private and public law of a given legal system.

supervision of the debtor's assets and affairs (even by requesting joint approval for sales of debtors' assets, as emerged in some protocols[52]); and (iii) approve protocols, where necessary. Courts should conform to such obligation even before the insolvency is declared:[53] the provision speaks of courts before which a 'request is pending'. This means, even though the state of insolvency has not been declared yet, courts already have an obligation to cooperate.

The regulation also makes reference to 'coordination of the conduct of hearings' (Article 43(3)(d)), which does not mean 'joined hearing'. Whereas the regulation provides courts with the possibility, for example, to schedule their own hearings in light of the development of foreign proceedings (and, if appropriate schedule 'parallel hearings'), the regulation does not grant courts the right to conduct joined hearings,[54] which thus remain possible only in so far as these are admitted by the laws of the different jurisdictions involved.

Parallel provisions are given for cooperation between insolvency office holders and courts[55] in proceedings opened against the same debtor (Article 43), and against companies party to a group (Article 58). Insolvency practitioners have an obligation to cooperate and communicate with foreign courts. This seems to create an obligation of cooperation of administrators with foreign courts, but not the other way around.[56] This particular wording of the provisions, however, finds some comfort in the circumstance that, usually, insolvency proceedings are mostly managed by administrators (which already have an obligation to cooperate), and in that administrators are automatically recognised in their quality in the European judicial space. Hence, liquidators of the main insolvency proceedings can request information to courts that have opened secondary proceedings, and secondary administrators can (at least[57]) ask for information to the principal administrator. With the important specification that, in case for proceedings opened against companies party to a group, an insolvency practitioner (without thus specifying if

---

[52] Cross-Border Insolvency Protocol AgriBioTech Canada, Inc., Article 2.01.

[53] Bork and Mangano 2016, p. 201; and Mankowski 2016a (Article 41), para 6.

[54] Moss and Smith 2016, p. 485.

[55] On the duty to cooperate between practitioners and courts, in the domestic law see §347(2) InsO, according to which foreign practitioners that have applied in Germany for provisional measures are under the obligation to inform the court of '*all essential changes in the foreign proceedings and of all further foreign insolvency proceedings known to him relating to the assets of the debtor*'.

[56] Speaking of 'unilateral duty', see Wessels 2015a (Cooperation), p. 787. See also Mankowski 2016c (Article 43), para 2.

[57] The 2013 UNCITRAL Model Law on Cross-Border Insolvency with Guide to Enactment and Interpretation suggests however a better and broader approach, as on recognition of a foreign proceedings, whether main or non-main, where necessary to protect the assets of the debtor or the interests of the creditors, the court may, at the request of the foreign representative, grant any appropriate relief, including the delivery of information concerning the debtor's assets, affairs, rights, obligations or liabilities (Article 21(a)(d)). Addressing the different scenarios, Mankowski 2016c (Article 43), para 5 ff.

this has been appointed in a principal or secondary proceedings[58]) '*may request information from that court concerning the proceedings regarding the other member of the group or request assistance concerning the proceedings in which he has been appointed*'.[59]

5.3.3   Cooperation and Communication: Sources of Practices

Where the content of the different obligations can only be identified through given examples, the regulation opens to soft law: recital 48 of the regulation paves the way to European and international 'best practices'.

The first question concerns the very definition of 'best practice' that can be taken into account in the context of the regulation. The Oxford Dictionaries define them as '[c]*ommercial or professional procedures that are accepted or prescribed as being correct or most effective*'. In this sense, (comparable[60]) practices should be of relevance only if their recourse is accepted as leading to a maximisation of the outcomes of the insolvency proceedings and are thus able to ingenerate a reasonable expectation that the practice at hand will be followed by all the parties. More surely, it seems that a practice should be classified as 'best practice' if a departure from this working method is not contested by practitioners only in so far as this is reasonably justified. If a practice acquires a 'comply or explain'[61] nature, this expresses the 'best practice' nature of the working method.

According to recital 48, interested parties are called to take into consideration 'best practices' as '*set out in principles and guidelines*' adopted by relevant organisations. The regulation itself mentions those developed by the United Nations Commission on International Trade Law (Uncitral), but there is little reason to doubt that the work of other groups, such as the TRI-Leiden or the INSOL Group, could provide a solid basis to detect good practices to be followed by the actors of cross-border insolvency proceedings. The question remains open whether any EU institution will adopt its own collection of best practices in the future, or at least endorse some of the already existing guidelines and principles, so as to better persuade all actors to comply with the principles enshrined therein.

---

[58] Cfr. Schmidt 2016b (Article 58), p. 604.

[59] EIR Recast, Article 58(b).

[60] Adriaanse et al. 2014, p. 38.

[61] Santen 2015, p. 235 f.

5.3.4 Statutory and Practical Limits to Cooperation and Communication

Strengthening cooperation duties amongst the interested parties could settle the need for coordination of multiple parallel proceedings and the specific interests of insolvency practitioners. Nonetheless, the current legal framework could fall short from its goal, as a number of both statutory and practical limits could run counter to the efficiency and effectiveness of the system.

Some obstacles to cooperation appear to be beyond the sphere of control and influence of the parties. In spite of that, most domestic and European Union law provisions, if properly interpreted and applied, might require effort, but still turn out to be effective in the end.

5.3.4.1 Statutory Limits

A general limit to cooperation and coordination is the compatibility of the various *lex processus* at stake. It is for the different laws of the concerned Member States to set the limits to cooperation.[62] All provisions clearly speak of '*non-incompatibility*', a double negative phrase that stresses that mere inconsistency between the laws should not trigger the exception to cooperation—which as such must be narrowly interpreted and applied.[63]

Of course, this statutory limit must be evaluated in light of practical data. Practitioners working in continental civil law legal systems have little experience with cross-border protocols and agreements. Continental courts in particular might be uncertain as to the extent to which their own domestic laws allow for cross-border cooperation and cooperation. A circumstance that is well exemplified in the understanding that '[m]*ost simply put, the common law with its ingredient of inherent jurisdiction allows judges to do what justice and the law requires, but also what practicality dictates* [...] *However, the tradition of the Civil Code is that the judiciary is only allowed to do what the Code specifically allows*'.[64] It thus falls upon the parties to explore, absent clear domestic legislation, their limits to cooperation—bearing in mind that local unclear or incomplete provisions should not deprive the regulation of its *effet utile*.

As mentioned before, another general limit—specific to exchange of information between practitioners—concerns the necessity to make arrangements to protect confidential information. What remains to be settled is what happens if such an agreement is not concluded, either because of a lack of consensus on the terms of

---

[62] EIR Recast, Article 41; Article 42; Article 43; Article 56; Article 57; Article 58.

[63] Also arguing for a restrictive interpretation on the limits to cooperation and communication, Bork and Mangano 2016, p. 289.

[64] Farley et al. 2006, p. 4; Maltese 2013, p. 363; Requejo Isidro 2016, p. 78; Paulus 2006, p. 1, and Koutsoukou 2016, p. 85.

the agreement, or on the necessity of the agreement itself.[65] The regulation does not offer the main practitioner an effective mechanism to ensure secondary administrators exchange of confidential information. In general, the regulation sets obligations, but no sanctions.[66] As a breach of the obligation constitutes a breach of professional duties, liability should be governed by the respective law and addressed before the court where the professional has been appointed.[67]

Cooperation duties between courts under Article 42 and Article 57 of the EIR Recast are subject to an additional requirement. Cooperation must be appropriate to facilitate the effective administration of the proceedings.[68] Moreover, and only for cooperation between courts in parallel proceedings opened against different debtors of a group of companies, cooperation must not entail a conflict of interests.[69] Of course, such an appropriateness test will highly depend upon the specificities of the single case. The provision should be applied by taking into consideration that, in general, cooperation between insolvency proceedings bears positive effects, thus any admissible departure therefrom should be considered to be an exception.

Direct communication between courts is also subject to the respect of procedural rights of the parties. In the eye of some authors,[70] the possibility for courts to communicate without the parties being given the chance to intervene could run against European standards of procedural rights such as Article 47 of the EU Charter, with the consequence that, within the context of the regulation, this should not take place.

Also, the appointment of an independent person or body to act as a filter for cooperation between courts is not without controversy. The provisions use the singular ('*individual*' or '*body*')—yet this should not be subject to an interpretation contrary to the spirit of the provision,[71] and should not lead to think that both courts must appoint the same person. This might in fact not be possible under the diverse substantive laws, or simply not practically possible.

---

[65] As noted by Mankowski 2016a (Article 41), para 13 ff, only 'relevant' information should be shared between the parties, as 'information overkill' is as dangerous as no information at all.

[66] Mankowski 2016a (Article 41), para 87 ff, Mäsch 2015b (Article 31), p. 1212 f, and Pannen and Riedermann 2007 (Article 31), p. 469.

[67] EIR Recast, Article 6. The action would be an action deriving directly from insolvency proceedings and closely linked with them.

[68] Schmidt 2016c (Article 56), p. 595. In this sense, and leaving aside here group coordination proceedings, it seems only natural that each principal insolvency office holder acts to ensure maximization of value of the assets of the company he or she is managing in the context of an insolvency procedure: only where a coordination between different debtors (where no 'super-principal' administrator can overstep a secondary one) is for the benefit of all, any form of coordination can take place.

[69] Such a difference seems consistent with—and justifiable under—the current legal framework that still treats companies party to a group as separate legal entities, each subject to its own principal procedure.

[70] Moss and Smith 2016, p. 484.

[71] Mankowski 2016b (Article 42), para 9.

5.3.4.2   Practical Limits and Issues

For any of the abovementioned duty, a number of practical problems might hinder effective and efficient cooperation.

In the first place, inconsistencies between procedural laws might pose problems to civil law practitioners and courts. Where documents must be produced in a given form or in a given language, practitioners and courts will have to coordinate to the maximum possible extent to make sure a document from the State of origin can also be used in foreign proceedings.

In the second place, as mentioned, the EIR Recast does set obligations, but no sanctions. The question thus remains who, given the absence of an 'enforcement procedure', is competent in case of breach of duties to surrender information if someone considers documents non-relevant for the purposes of the provision; connected to a conflict of interests[72] or contrary to an efficient administration of parallel proceedings. Given that such questions are connected to professional liability and connected to insolvency proceedings, jurisdiction and applicable should be determined accordingly.

In the third place, language and legal insolvency terminology[73] might slow down communications, or make it less efficient and more costly. Communication should take place in a language that is known to all the parties[74] involved in the proceedings. Should this not be possible, an independent person acting on behalf of the court can be appointed.[75] If written agreements or protocols are concluded, these could offer a list of definitions,[76] so as also to avoid *faux amis*[77] and legal expressions encompassing different legal concepts in different jurisdictions. Despite the importance of the matter, language is taken into express consideration (only) in Article 73, which is devoted to 'group coordination procedures', one of the main new features of the regulation. This provision, even if contained in a different section of the act, very well could turn out as a guiding principle: according to Article 73, '*The coordinator shall communicate with the insolvency practitioner of a participating group member in the language agreed with the insolvency practitioner or, in the absence of an agreement, in the official language or one of the official languages of the institutions of the Union, and of the court which opened the proceedings in respect of that group member. The coordinator shall communicate with a court in the official language applicable to that court*'.

---

[72] Cfr. Wessels 2016b (Article 43), p. 501.

[73] As determined by practical investigations, practitioners have reported doubts and problems, in particular concerning the use of language and the lack of knowledge of accepted best practices. On the point, see Queirolo and Dominelli 2017a (Cooperation), p. 121.

[74] Addressing the issue, unsettled under the specific provision for cooperation between insolvency office holders, Mankowski 2016a (Article 41), para 31.

[75] Schmidt 2016a (Article 57), p. 600, and Wessels 2015b (A Glimpse), p. 99 f.

[76] Koutsoukou 2016, p. 92.

[77] Farley 2009, p. 81.

5.4   Form of Cooperation

According to recital 49 of the regulation, '*insolvency practitioners and courts should be able to enter into agreements and protocols for the purpose of facilitating cross-border cooperation of multiple insolvency proceedings in different Member States*'. No specific tool for cooperation is imposed, and a principle of 'freedom of forms', sometimes necessary[78] to incentivise practitioners and to cope with fragmentation of substantive and procedural law in the different Member States, is followed.

It seems that the regulation, and in particular Article 41, which clearly states that '[…] *cooperation may take any form, including the conclusion of agreements or protocols*' might be a sufficient legal basis for practitioners to enter such agreements absent a specific rule in their relevant domestic law.[79] However, the general limit of compatibility with national rules remains. The form by which cooperation is pursued is thus relevant as regards the precondition to cooperation itself. As cooperation is only possible insofar as this is not incompatible with the rules applicable to the respective proceedings, the more formal an agreement on cooperation is, the more limits it might encounter. Whereas it is impossible (both in legal, and practical terms) to reach an agreement, and to make it binding upon the interested parties, administrators are at least encouraged to pursue informal cooperation between themselves.

Agreements in general, and regardless of their nature and structure, can cover any matter, the only limit being the preservation of the *effet util* of the provision.[80]

It must however be noted that in continental Member States, practitioners and courts are not particularly used to cross-border cooperation, especially if this involves a practitioner and a foreign court, the latter being sometimes unsure of the limits for their cooperation.[81] Of course, the situation is different for common law countries, actors here being more inclined and more willing to cooperate at different levels with foreign counterparts,[82] where protocols or agreements ensure a better coordinated[83] and less adversarial[84] cross-border management of an insolvency case.

---

[78] Moss and Smith 2016, p. 482 f.

[79] Bork and Mangano 2016, p. 211.

[80] Mäsch 2015b (Article 31), p. 1210, and Mankowski 2016a (Article 41), para 2. In the context of the new regulation, see also Koutsoukou 2016, p. 88.

[81] With specific regard to the legal system, drawing up protocols consistent with the limits imposed by German law, see Busch et al. 2010, p. 28. Cf. also Bewick 2015, p. 184.

[82] On the possibilities for UK courts to cooperate with foreign courts, see Omar 2019, p. 119 ff.

[83] Due to the existence of possible multiples procedures, albeit different in nature (cfr. Esplugues Mota 2015, p. 389).

[84] *Expert Committee's Report on Cross-Border Insolvency Access and Recognition, Joint Project of UNCITRAL and INSOL International on Cross-Border Insolvencies*, in *International Insolvency Review*, 1996, p. 140, at p. 151. Cf. Virgós and Garcimartín 2004, p. 225.

As regards the nature of such instruments, it seems possible to identify two main categories, both mentioned, but not defined by the regulation, i.e. agreements and protocols. According to the United Nations Commission on International Trade Law, 'agreements' are *'oral or written agreement[s] intended to facilitate the coordination of cross-border insolvency proceedings and cooperation between courts, between courts and insolvency representatives and between insolvency representatives, sometimes also involving other parties in interest'*.[85] The term 'protocols' is also often used in practice, sometimes to indicate that courts enter an agreement, or to approve and incorporate an agreement in a court order.[86] Both protocols and agreements may vary in form and content, being possibly specific,[87] or generic—the terminology being used in the regulation in a flexible and broad way so as to encompass any form of cooperation.[88]

More important appears the classification in regards to their nature, more specifically whether or not such agreements are incorporated in a court order. If agreements are incorporated in court orders, they shall be treated as such, a failure to comply to the agreement becoming a failure to comply with a court order. If protocols are not incorporated in court orders, such agreements must be characterised[89] as contractual or insolvency for the proper identification of applicable law and heads of jurisdiction. Insolvency protocols appear strictly connected to insolvency proceedings, as a judicial enforcement would not be possible without the opening of insolvency proceedings. On the other hand, some of the obligations contained in the agreement might be qualified as 'obligations freely taken by the parties' as required by the case law of the Court of Justice of the European Union to classify an obligation as 'contractual' in nature.

5.5 Companies Party to a Group: A New Legal Framework

As seen, the insolvency regulation extends cooperation duties also between main practitioners of insolvency proceedings opened against different debtors of a group of companies. However, cooperation can also pursue a different path. Without

---

[85] UNCITRAL Practice Guide on Cross-Border Insolvency Cooperation, New York, 2010, p. 4.

[86] Koutsoukou 2016, p. 85; and Wessels 2012, p. 359 ff.

[87] Looking at the practices developed in the last years, it can be noted that the first protocols mainly wished to tackle communication and cooperation issues, whilst protocols, such as the Lehman and the Madoff, developed in the context of the crisis of financial companies, were more specific in that they had detailed (non-binding) principles for creditors' rights, intercompany claims, and other substantive aspects (see Fumagalli 2018, p. 181).

[88] Koutsoukou 2016, p. 86.

[89] Tackling the issue as regards the law applicable to agreements concluded by insolvency office holders, see Hess 2010, p. 525; Wessels 2012, para 7; Mankowski 2016a (Article 41), para 53 ff.; Bork and Mangano 2016, p. 211; and Vallar 2017, p. 133 f.

creating a "super-insolvency proceedings", i.e. a single insolvency proceedings for all independent companies of a group, the EIR Recast introduces new rules for 'coordination' of such multiple and autonomous insolvency proceedings. Rules which are without prejudice to the competence of the court to open main proceedings against the company of a group if the courts determines the COMI within its jurisdiction.[90] Most importantly, the scheme of 'coordination' is grounded on the principle of voluntary participation.

The goal of a group coordination proceedings is to identify a person whose duty it is to develop recommendations or a group coordination plan.[91] A duty that might turn out to be difficult, because, other than the matter of costs, the coordination procedure in general might be sought most probably where practitioners are already unable to reach cooperation under their general obligations.[92] The coordinator *shall* (i) identify and outline recommendations for the coordinated conduct of the insolvency proceedings; (ii) propose a group coordination plan[93] that identifies, describes and recommends a comprehensive set of measures appropriate to an integrated approach to the resolution of the group members' insolvencies (such as measures, fundamental in cases of rehabilitation plans,[94] to be taken in order to re-establish the economic performance and the financial soundness of the group or any part of it; settlement of intra-group disputes as regards intra-group transactions and avoidance actions; agreements between the insolvency practitioners of the insolvent group members).[95] Additionally, the coordinator *may* (i) be heard and participate in any of the proceedings opened in respect of any member of the group; (ii) mediate any dispute arising between two or more insolvency practitioners; (iii) present and explain the group coordination plan; (iv) request information from any insolvency practitioner (thus not directly to courts before which the proceeding is pending) in respect of any member of the group where that information is or might be of use when identifying and outlining strategies and measures in order to coordinate the proceedings; (v) request a stay for a period of up to 6 months of the proceedings opened in respect of any member of the group, provided that such a stay is necessary in order to ensure the proper implementation of the plan and would be to the benefit of the creditors in the proceedings for which the stay is requested.[96]

The coordinator, which must be eligible to be an insolvency practitioner under the law of any Member State (thus not necessarily under the law of the Member

---

[90] EIR Recast, recital 53.

[91] Schmidt 2016d (Article 61), para 11.

[92] Thole and Dueñas 2016, p. 220.

[93] Excluding however recommendations as to any consolidation of proceedings or insolvency estates (EIR Recast, Article 72(3)). In favour of this option Thole and Dueñas 2016, p. 219. On the other hand, consolidation of assets has also been taken into consideration by some, and sometimes taken into consideration by practitioners.

[94] Moss and Smith 2016, p. 515.

[95] EIR Recast, Article 72(1).

[96] *Ibidem*, Article 72(2).

State of habitual residence), and not being already appointed in relation to an insolvency proceedings of the companies party to a group[97] (so as to ensure neutrality[98]), is appointed by one court to which request to open a group coordination proceedings is lodged.[99] The request to open such a procedure, lodged by any insolvency practitioner of any of the companies party to a group in accordance with the national law of the practitioner lodging the request,[100] is accompanied by a proposal as to the person to be nominated as coordinator, an outline of the proposed group coordination (also necessary for other liquidators to take an informed choice[101]), a list of the insolvency practitioners appointed in relation to the members of the group and, where relevant, the courts and competent authorities involved, and an outline of the estimated costs of the proposed group coordination and the estimation of the share of those costs to be paid by each member of the group. The court seised will give notice as soon as possible of the request and of the proposed coordinator to the insolvency practitioners appointed in relation to all[102] members of the group (regardless of whether it is apparent that one company will not take part in the group procedure) if the court believes that the group procedure is appropriate to facilitate the effective administration of the insolvency proceedings. The final decision of the participation rests with the coordinator, whose decision can be appealed before the court before which the procedure has been opened.

Not only participation to the procedure is voluntary in nature, but also compliance to the coordinator's recommendation is. The regulation introduces a 'complain or explain' rule[103] as it clearly states that '[a]n *insolvency practitioner shall not be obliged to follow in whole or in part the coordinator's recommendations or the group coordination plan. If it does not follow the coordinator's recommendations or the group coordination plan, it shall give reasons for not doing so to the persons or bodies that it is to report to under its national law, and to the coordinator'.*[104]

---

[97] *Ibidem*, Article 71.

[98] *Ibidem*, Article 72(5).

[99] *Ibidem*, Article 61. In favour of this solution, which maintains flexibility, Thole and Dueñas 2016, p. 223, even though acknowledging that this might lead to a certain forum shopping as regards the choice of the court competent for the group procedure.

[100] EIR Recast, Article 61(2), on which see Bork and Mangano 2016, p. 291; and Schmidt 2016d (Article 61), para 18.

[101] Schmidt 2016d (Article 61), para 37 ff., also highlighting the different linguistic versions of the regulation on this very point.

[102] Schmidt 2016d (Article 61), para 45.

[103] Thole and Dueñas 2016, p. 218; and Schmidt 2016e (Article 70), para 2.

[104] EIR Recast, Article 70(2).

5.6 Final Remarks

Other than the already addressed statutory and practical limits, exchange of information, coordination, and cooperation is strictly interconnected with the skills and abilities of practitioners, which are determined by domestic laws. It is apparent that requirements to exercise the function of insolvency practitioner should converge between Member States.[105] Common ethical standards are a necessity to ensure proper implementation of the regulation. In this specific field, best practices have been collected for example by TRI Leiden[106] or by the European Bank for Reconstruction and Development.[107] It seems not only practitioners should individually adhere to such principles on a voluntary basis, but also professional orders, if not domestic legislators, should adopt binding rules to ensure compliance, throughout the whole European judicial space, to such common ethic and professional standards.

References

Adriaanse JAA, Wuisman I, Santen B (2014) European Principles and Best Practices for Insolvency Office Holders, Report II: A Comparative Analysis of Rules for Insolvency Office Holder in Eleven European Countries as a Means to Identify Room for Principles and Best Practices. https://www.researchgate.net/publication/292151187_European_Principles_and_Best_Practices_for_Insolvency_Office_Holders_Report_II_A_Comparative_Analysis_of_Rules_for_Insolvency_Office_Holders_in_Eleven_European_Countries_as_a_Means_to_Identify_Room_fo (Accessed 21 March 2019)
Arnold M (2015) The Insolvency Regulation. In: Sheldon R (ed). Cross-Border Insolvency. Bloomsbury, London, pp 16–111
Bewick S (2015) The EU Insolvency Regulation, Revisited. International Insolvency Review 24:172–191
Bork R (2017) Principles of Cross-Border Insolvency Law. Intersentia, Cambridge
Bork R, Mangano R (2016) European Cross-Border Insolvency Law. Oxford University Press, Oxford
Busch P, Remmert A, Rüntz S, Vallender H (2010) Kommunikation zwischen Gerichten in grenzüberschreitenden Insolvenzen - Was geht und was nicht geht [Communication between courts in cross-border insolvencies – What works and what does not]. Neue Zeitschrift für Insolvenz- und Sanierungsrecht [New Review for insolvency and rescue law] 13:417–430

---

[105] European Parliament Draft Report with recommendations to the Commission on insolvency proceedings in the context of EU company law (2011/2006(INI).

[106] 2015 INSOL Europe Statement of Principles and Guidelines for Insolvency Office Holders in Europe, available online, on which see Wessels 2015c, p. 757 ff. See also INSOL Europe—Insolvency Office Holders Forum, Report on the Regulation of Insolvency Office Holders, 2016, available online.

[107] 2007 European Bank for Reconstruction and Development, Principles in Respect of the Qualifications, Appointment, Conduct, Supervision, and Regulation of Office Holders in Insolvency Cases, available online.

Carbone SM (2004) Il Regolamento (CE) n. 1346/2000 relativo alle procedure di insolvenza [Regulation (EC) n. 1346/2000 on cross-border insolvency]. In: Carbone SM, Frigo M, Fumagalli L (eds) Diritto processuale civile e commerciale comunitario [Community procedural law in civil and commercial matters]. Giuffré, Milan, pp 89–117

Crawford E, Carruthers J (2015) International Private Law: A Scots Perspective. W. Green, Edinburgh

Daniele L (1987) Il fallimento nel diritto internazionale privato e processuale [Insolvency in private and procedural international law]. CEDAM, Padua

Enriques G (1934) Universalità e territorialità del fallimento nel diritto internazionale privato [Universality and territoriality of insolvency in private international law]. Rivista di diritto internazionale [International law journal] 16:145–170

Esplugues Mota C (2015) Procedimientos de insolvencia transfronterizos [Cross-border insolvency proceedings]. In: Esplugues Mota C (ed) Derecho del Comercio Internacional [The law of international commerce]. Tirant, Valencia, pp 379–402

Farley J (2009) A practical Approach to Court-to-Court Communication in International Insolvency Law (reporters Viimsalu S, Weber J). In: Verweij A, Wessels B (eds) INSOL Europe Technical Series – Comparative and International Insolvency Law Central Thoughts and Themes – Papers from the Honours Class 'Comparative and International Insolvency Law' organised at Leiden Law School. INSOL Europe, Nottingham, pp 76–82

Farley J (1997) Joint UNCITRAL/INSOL Judicial Colloquium on Cross-Border Insolvency (New Orleans, March 1997) Judges' Evaluation - Collective Report. International Insolvency Review 6:236–251

Farley J, Leonard B, Birch J (2006) International Annual Regional Conference Cooperation and Coordination in Cross-Border Insolvency Cases. https://www.iiiglobal.org/sites/default/files/JMFarley.pdf (Accessed 27 March 2019)

Fazzini P (2015) Promulgato il nuovo regolamento (UE) N. 2015/848 sulle procedure di insolvenza transfrontaliere: principali profili di riforma [The new Regulation (EU) N. 2015/848 on cross-border insolvency proceedings: main reforms]. Diritto del commercio internazionale [Law journal of international commerce] 29:907–916

Fumagalli L (2018) I protocolli tra le procedure nella disciplina transfrontaliera dell'insolvenza [Protocols in cross-border insolvency proceedings]. In: Leandro A, Meo G, Nuzzo A (eds) Crisi Transfrontaliera di impresa: orizzonti internazionali ed europei [Transnational crisis of companies: international and European horizons]. Cacucci, Bari, pp 181–197

Hess B (2010) Europäisches Zivilprozessrecht [European civil procedure]. C.F. Muller, Heidelberg

Israël J (2005) European Cross-Border Insolvency Regulation. A Study of Regulation 1346/2000 on Insolvency Proceedings in the Light of a Paradigm of Cooperation and a Comitas Europaea. Intersentia, Antwerp

Kindler P (2018) Einleitung [Introduction]. In: Münchener Kommentar zum Bürgerlichen Gesetzbuch [Munich commentary on the civil code], Band 12. Beck Verlag, Munich, pp 1931–1940

Koutsoukou G (2016) Part 2: Cooperation Between Main and Secondary Proceedings – Protocols, in the Implementation of the New Insolvency Regulation, Recommendations and Guidelines. Study JUST/2013/JCIV/AG/4679. http://insreg.mpi.lu/Guidelines.pdf (Accessed 27 March 2019)

Laukemann B (2016) Regulatory Copy and Paste: The Allocation of Assets in Crossborder Insolvencies – Methodological Perspectives from the Nortel Decision. Journal of Private International Law 12:379–410

Leandro A (2014) Amending the European Insolvency Regulation to Strengthen Main Proceedings. Rivista di diritto internazionale privato e processuale 50:317–340

Leandro A (2017) Insolvency, Cooperation and Recognition. In: Basedow J, Rühl G, Ferrari F, De Miguel Asensio P (eds). Encyclopedia of Private International Law, Vol. II. Edward Elgar, Cheltenham, pp 939–947

Leandro A (2018) Procedure secondarie 'sintetiche' e diritto applicabile nella procedura principale [Summary secondary proceedings and applicable law in the main proceedings]. In: Leandro A, Meo G, Nuzzo A (eds) Crisi Transfrontaliera di impresa: orizzonti internazionali ed europei [Transnational crisis of companies: international and European horizons]. Cacucci, Bari, pp 119–134

Lupone A (1995) L'insolvenza transnazionale: Procedure concorsuali nello Stato e beni all'estero [Transnational insolvency: collective proceedings in the State and assets located abroad]. CEDAM, Padua

Maltese M (2013) Le forme di cooperazione internazionale nelle procedure di insolvenza transfrontaliera [Forms of international cooperation in transnational insolvency proceedings]. In: Carbone SM (ed) L'Unione europea a vent'anni da Maastricht: verso nuove regole [The European Union: twenty years after the Maastricht Treaty]. Editoriale scientifica, Naples, pp 341–366

Mankowski P (2016a) Art. 41 Zusammenarbeit und Kommunikation der Verwalter [Art. 41 Cooperation and communication between insolvency practitioners]. In: Mankowski P, Müller M, Schmidt J (eds) EuInsVO 2015 [EU Insolvency Regulation 2015]. Beck Verlag, Munich, para 1–106

Mankowski P (2016b) Art. 42 Zusammenarbeit und Kommunikation der Gerichte [Art 42 Cooperation and communication between courts]. In: Mankowski P, Müller M, Schmidt J (eds) EuInsVO 2015 [EU Insolvency Regulation]. Beck Verlag, Munich, para 1–30

Mankowski P (2016c) Art. 43 Zusammenarbeit und Kommunikation zwischen Verwaltern und Gerichten [Art 43 Cooperation and communication between insolvency practitioners and courts]. In: Mankowski P, Müller M, Schmidt J (eds) EuInsVO 2015 [EU Insolvency Regulation 2015]. Beck Verlag, Munich, para 1–13

Mäsch G (2015a) Einleitung [Introduction]. In: Rauscher T (ed) Europäisches Zivilprozess- und Kollisionsrecht EuZPR/EuIPR, Band II [European civil procedure and conflict of laws, Volume II]. Otto Schmidt Verlag, Cologne, pp 1069–1074

Mäsch G (2015b) Art. 31 EG-InsVO [Art 31 EU Insolvency Regulation]. In: Rauscher T (ed) Europäisches Zivilprozess- und Kollisionsrecht EuZPR/EuIPR, Band II [European civil procedure and conflict of laws, Volume II]. Otto Schmidt Verlag, Cologne, pp 1208–1214

McCormack G (2015) Something Old, Something New: Recasting the European Insolvency Regulation. The Modern Law Review 79:102–146

Moss G, Smith T (2016) Commentary on Regulation 1346/2000 and Recast Regulation 2015/848 on Insolvency Proceedings. In: Moss G, Fletcher I, Isaacs S (eds) Moss, Fletcher and Isaacs on the EU Regulation on Insolvency Proceedings. Oxford University Press, Oxford, para 8.01–8.823

Oberhammer P, Koller C, Auernig K, Planitzer L (2016) Part 3: Insolvencies of Groups of Companies, in the Implementation of the New Insolvency Regulation, Recommendations and Guidelines. Study JUST/2013/JCIV/AG/4679. http://insreg.mpi.lu/Guidelines.pdf (Accessed 27 March 2019)

Omar P (2019) UK Cross-Border Cooperation: Extending Rescue to Jersey Debtors on a 'Passporting' Basis. International Insolvency Review 22:119–143

Pannen K, Riedermann S (2007) Artikel 31 [Article 31]. In: Pannen K (ed) Europäische Insolvenzverordnung: Kommentar [The European Insolvency Regulation: a commentary]. de Gruyter, Berlin, pp 457–470

Paulus C (2006) Judicial Cooperation in Cross-Border Insolvencies: An outline of some relevant issues and literature. http://siteresources.worldbank.org/GILD/Resources/GJF2006Judicial CooperationinInsolvency_PaulusEN.pdf (Accessed 27 March 2019)

Paulus C (2017) EuInsVo. Europäische Insolvenzverordnung, Kommentar [The EU Insolvency Regulation: a commentary]. Beck Verlag, Frankfurt am Main

Queirolo I (2007) Le procedure d'insolvenza nella disciplina comunitaria: Modelli di riferimento e diritto interno [Insolvency proceedings in community law: reference models and domestic law]. Giappichelli, Turin

Queirolo I, Dominelli S (2017a) Cooperation between Authorities and Insolvency Office Holders. In: Queirolo I, Dominelli S (eds) European and National Perspectives on the European Insolvency Regulation. Aracne, Rome, pp 117–185

Queirolo I, Dominelli S (2017b) Italian Report on Cross-Border Insolvency Proceedings: Detecting Best Practices. In: Queirolo I, Dominelli S (eds) European and National Perspectives on the European Insolvency Regulation. Aracne, Rome, pp 315–355

Requejo Isidro M (2016) Part 2: Cooperation Between Main and Secondary Proceedings – Cooperation, Communication, Coordination, in the Implementation of the New Insolvency Regulation, Recommendations and Guidelines. Study JUST/2013/JCIV/AG/4679. http://insreg.mpi.lu/Guidelines.pdf (Accessed 27 March 2019)

Santen B (2015) Communication and Cooperation in International Insolvency: On Best Practices for Insolvency for Office Holders and Cross-Border Communication Between Courts. ERA Forum 16:229–240

Schmidt J (2016a) Art. 56 – Cooperation and Communication Between Insolvency Practitioners. In: Bork R, van Zwieten K (eds) Commentary on the European Insolvency Regulation. Oxford University Press, Oxford, para 56.01–56.30

Schmidt J (2016b) Art. 57 – Cooperation and Communication Between Courts. In: Bork R, van Zwieten K (eds) Commentary on the European Insolvency Regulation. Oxford University Press, Oxford, para 57.01–57.21

Schmidt J (2016c) Art. 58 – Cooperation and Communication between Insolvency Practitioners and Courts. In: Bork R, van Zwieten K (eds) Commentary on the European Insolvency Regulation. Oxford University Press, Oxford, para 58.01–58.09

Schmidt J (2016d) Art. 61 Antrag auf Eröffnung eines Gruppen-Koordinationsverfahrens [Art 61 Request to open group coordination proceedings]. In: Mankowski P, Müller M, Schmidt J (eds) EuInsVO 2015 [European Insolvency Regulation 2015]. Beck Verlag, Munich, para 1–50

Schmidt J (2016e) Art. 70 Empfehlungen und Gruppen-Koordinationsplan [Recommendations and group coordination plan]. In: Mankowski P, Müller M, Schmidt J (eds) EuInsVO 2015 [European Insolvency Regulation 2015]. Beck Verlag, Munich, para 1–23

Schmüser G (2009) Das Zusammenspiel zwischen Haupt- und Sekundärinsolvenzverfahren nach der EuInsVo [The interplay between the main and secondary insolvency proceedings in the EU Insolvency Regulation]. Peter Lang Verlag, Frankfurt Am Main

Shandro S (1998) Judicial Co-operation in Cross-Border Insolvency - The English Court Takes a Step Backwards in BCCI (Np. 10). International Insolvency Review 7:63–78

Starace V (2002) La disciplina comunitaria delle procedure di insolvenza: giurisdizione ed efficacia delle sentenze straniere. Rivista di diritto internazionale 85:295–308

Thole C, Dueñas M (2016) Some Observations on the New Group Coordination Procedure of the Reformed European Insolvency Regulation. International Insolvency Review 24:214–227

Vallar G (2017) La crisi dei gruppi bancari multinazionali. Metodi di diritto internazionale privato e coordinamento tra sistemi [Insolvency of multinational banking groups. Conflict of laws methods and coordination of systems]. Giuffré, Milan

Van Calster G (2016) COMIng, and Here to Stay: The Review of the European Insolvency Regulation. European Business Law Review 27:735–753

Villata FC (2018) Determinazione del COMI e libertà di stabilimento delle società nell'Unione europea [Determination of COMI and right of establishment of companies within the European Union]. In: Leandro A, Meo G, Nuzzo A (eds) Crisi Transfrontaliera di impresa: orizzonti internazionali ed europei [Transnational crisis of companies: international and European horizons]. Cacucci, Bari, pp 83–101

Virgós M, Garcimartín F (2004) The European Insolvency Regulation: Law and Practice. Kluwer Law, The Hague

Wessels B (2012) Cross-border Insolvency Agreements: What Are They and Are They Here to Stay? http://www.bobwessels.nl/site/assets/files/1405/cross-border-agreements-nijmegen-final.pdf (Accessed 27 March 2019)

Wessels B (2015a) A Glimpse into the Future: Cross-border Judicial Cooperation in Insolvency Cases in the European Union. International Insolvency Review 24:96–121

Wessels B (2015b) Cooperation and Sharing of Information Between Courts and Insolvency Practitioners in Cross-Border Insolvency Cases. In: Graf-Schlicker ML, Uhlenbruck W, Prütting H (eds) Festschrift für Heinz Vallender. de Gruyter, Tuebingen, pp 775–792

Wessels B (2015c) Harmonisation of Requirements for Insolvency Holders on a European Level. In: Bork R, Kayser G, Kebekus F (eds) Festschrift für Bruno M. Kübler zum 70. Geburtstag. Beck Verlag, Munich, pp 757–772

Wessels B (2016a) Art. 41 – Cooperation and Communication Between Insolvency Practitioners. In: Bork R, van Zwieten K (eds) Commentary on the European Insolvency Regulation. Oxford University Press, para 41.01–41.16

Wessels B (2016b) Art. 43 – Cooperation and Communication Between Insolvency Practitioners and Courts. In: Bork R, van Zwieten K (eds) Commentary on the European Insolvency Regulation. Oxford University Press, para 43.01–43.07

Wessels B, Virgós M (2007) INSOL Europe, European Communication and Cooperation Guidelines for Cross-Border Insolvency. https://www.insol-europe.org/publications/technical-series-publications (Accessed 27 March 2019)